To my beautiful grandchildren. May you always have Jesus in your hearts as your source of hope.

Contents

Foreword.. ix

A Note to You xi

Section One

Standing in the Storms: Drenched in Struggles.................. 13

    Choices 15

    Finding Peace in the Pain 25

    Accepting God's Promises:

    Only Hope in the Storm 37

Section Two

Singing in the Rain: Drenched in Survival......................... 45

    Perseverance 47

    Forgiveness... 61

    Clothed in God's Grace: Endless Hope.................... 71

Section Three

Splashing in the Puddles: Drenched in His Splendor 81

    Refreshing Rest 83

    Worship 93

    Basking in God's Provisions:

    Drenched in Hope 107

Section Four

Sharing under the Rainbow: Drenched in *Son*shine 117

    Misery to Ministry 121

    Sweet Encouragement 129

    Sharing God's Love: Living Letters of Hope 139

Afterword 145

Recommended Reading 147

Giving Thanks: Drenched in Gratitude 149

How to Hear the Songs 151

About the Author 153

Foreword

I love this book. The title draws the reader in. I love the visuals it brings to the mind. The stories in this book will walk you through a lot of painful events. The Scriptures will show you the power of God to transform pain by his protection and provision. I love the intertwining songs throughout the book.

Debbie has gone through many brutal events in life, but the main focus of this book is what *God* does. The biblical promises related throughout *Drenched* create freedom instead of fear, grace instead of guilt. People will be blessed by reading this book! The writing style and life experiences are easy to relate to. This book will bring healing.

In His Service,
Charles Gerber

A Note to You

The wind and waves are wild and high. The dark clouds roll in. The storm moves in and takes over your strength. A dangerous undercurrent pulls you out into the deep water, and you feel as though you will sink. What storms are causing you to drown:

- Pain caused by cancer or other disease
- Unresolved trauma from rape or abuse
- Anger over betrayal or broken relationships
- Grief over death or loss
- Guilt from sin

You try to swim on your own but can't seem to keep your head above the raging waves. Just when your body gives way, someone wraps his arms around you and carries you through the rough waters and onto the shore. You notice a brightness in the distance and see the beautiful sunset appearing below the storm clouds. Something good is on the way:

- Comfort
- Protection

- Peace
- Rest
- Love

God can carry you through all the difficult trials of life. Rest in his arms and allow him to take you on a journey.

God is the only hope in the storm.

Standing in the Storms: Drenched in Struggles

Water skiing. All of us kids wanted to learn to water ski. My older siblings had already learned the art of skiing and riding on a homemade surfboard and disc. On summer weekends, our family would travel to a campground with a small lake in north central Indiana. My brother and I, the two youngest, were only allowed to ride in the speedboat and watch our siblings and their friends ski.

We enjoyed sliding down the tall slide into the roped-off swimming area, feasting on chicken and noodles cooked on the camper stove (for some reason they tasted totally different from the ones cooked at home), watching the aluminum foil top poof up on the popcorn being cooked over the campfire, and riding our bikes with other kids over dirt piles at the back of the campground.

But around six years old, watching others waterski wasn't enough anymore. I wanted to be out on the water myself. I told Dad I wanted to learn. Truthfully, I didn't just want to.

I ached to soar over the water like my siblings. When Dad said if I proved to him I could swim he would teach me, I was thrilled.

Out we went to a quiet section of the lake, where, with a little push, I jumped from the side of the speedboat so Dad could judge my swimming ability. Even though I knew I wasn't the best swimmer, my desire to learn along with a strong trust in my father's presence allowed me to somehow keep my head above water. Ultimately, my confidence came from knowing my father's love. Soon I was gliding through the water on skis instead of always riding in the boat.

I had made the choice to learn to ski. That choice led to some rough going at first, but I trusted my father to protect me through the learning stages and help me be successful. In the same way, different choices made in life (either by ourselves or by others) can bring problems and struggles, but our loving heavenly Father is trustworthy. He can help us find peace, even in the midst of pain.

Choices

You must make a choice to take a chance, or your life will never change.

—Unknown

Imagine strolling in the sunshine, your smile bright, face warm, ears enjoying the sounds of nature around you. Without warning, the wind picks up, and dark clouds roll in. You are caught in the middle of a downpour without your umbrella. Your hair is plastered to your face, and your clothing—now cold, wet, and stuck fast to your skin—becomes less protection and more a problem. As you slosh through the rapidly rising water, shoes becoming waterlogged, every step is heavier. You are drenched. Winds blow sideways, pushing you faster than you want to go. You can barely see where you are walking through the heavy drops of rain. Saturated, you feel as though you are caught in a flood.

In May 1978, someone called me toward shelter from my storm. This was when I made the choice to take a chance for my life to change. I made the most important choice I had ever made—or will ever make—in my life.

A coworker at the bank where I worked invited me to audition for a play at a community theatre. She thought since I could sing I could act. (I had never been in a play, let alone a musical. The auditions alone were a strange experience.) Looking for time away from a relationship gone bad, I thought rehearsals would at least keep me busy. What my coworker didn't realize was that I was in a storm of my own—a flood—drenched in struggles and pain, trying to tread water and keep from drowning.

Standing in front of a panel of strangers, I performed "On a Clear Day You Can See Forever." Not bad. Then I was asked to read a selected portion from a script.

"You brood of vipers! Who warned you to flee from the coming wrath?"[1] What? Thoughts sped through my mind. What was this play about anyway? Where were these words from, and who talked like this? Sadly, I pronounced "You brood of vipers!" as "You broad of vipers!" Small snickers trickled from the other hopefuls waiting for their turn, and I had no clue why. Did I mention the play was *Godspell*, a musical using some of the parables of Jesus from the book of Matthew in the Bible? I had never read the Bible and hadn't a clue what the words meant, let alone how to pronounce them.

One audition became a callback. That callback became a second callback. Thinking this was the most ridiculous thing I had ever pursued, I spent my time in callback auditions giggling, unable to accomplish most of what the director asked.

---

1.   Originally, this is from Matthew 3:7, but John-Michael Tebelak made it part of his script for *Godspell*.

Over one hundred actors auditioned for thirteen parts. You guessed it! I was chosen as one of the thirteen. The director apparently liked my bubbly, giggly attitude, even though I had no idea what this play was about.

Had I never made the choice to step totally out of my comfort zone and audition for a play I knew nothing about, I would never have met my future husband, a man who loved Jesus and helped me see how important God would be in my life. Through that experience, God took a broken-down, confused, tired-of-relationships nineteen-year-old girl under the shelter of his wings and showed me the warmth of compassion, comfort, love, and, most of all, hope for eternity.

He did all this because, long before, God made a choice of his own. He chose to create me.

> For you created my inmost being;
> you knit me together in my mother's womb.
> I praise you because I am fearfully and wonderfully made;
> your works are wonderful,
> I know that full well.
> My frame was not hidden from you
> when I was made in the secret place,
> when I was woven together in the depths of the earth.
> Your eyes saw my unformed body;
> all the days ordained for me were written in your book
> before one of them came to be.
> (Psalm 139:13–16)

Even with the knowledge that I had made the best decision ever, life moved quickly after the play. I started dating my future husband, became engaged, and married him the following year. In 1980, we began a "brood" of our own and eventually had four beautiful children. My husband entered youth ministry, which included its own set of joys, pressures, and disappointments, but we did our best.

However, by the time we settled into our third local church, at thirty years of age, I found myself feeling unhappy, depressed, angry, worthless as a wife and mother . . . and suicidal.

At this church in Hillsboro, Ohio, I experienced an awful betrayal. I found that someone I thought was sent as an angel—someone who I felt was throwing me a lifeline in the midst of my flood—wanted to rob me of something else: my family. When this storm broke, I was too vulnerable.

Overwhelmed by anger and confusion, I finally reached out to a Christian counselor. In the sessions, I sifted through my past and realized several events—including abuse, rape, and the emotions caused by them—had lain dormant for many years and were only now coming to the surface. With the storm raging in my present and the dam breaking from my past, I was pounded from every side.

Finding myself in the midst of a rushing flood, drenched and beaten in the struggle, my façade of being the wonderful wife, mother, and youth minister's wife was knocked off and broken to bits. My suppressed past of abuse had caught up with me. Feeling useless and worthless, I clung to past pain, and that pain saturated my total being and all areas of my life. I went through the motions of daily life but could barely function.

Trying to stand in the raging waters and storms of life while pretending to enjoy the sun simply doesn't work. Choosing to acknowledge our storms is the first step toward allowing God to bring us into a warm, dry shelter and heal our hearts.

Without a doubt, I (and probably you) can absolutely agree with Jesus when he said, "In this world you will have trouble" (John 16:33). What troubles, struggles, and events cause pain in your life:

Abortion

Abuse

Addictions

Adolescent rebellion

Adultery

Aging

Betrayal

Broken-down car

Bullying

Car accident

Church conflict

Daily grind of life

Death

Depression

Disabilities

Disappointment

Disasters (like 9/11)

Diseases

Divorce

Eating disorders

Empty nest

Exhaustion

Failure

Fatigue

Financial stress

Gossip

Grief

Guilt

Hate

Hypocrisy

Illness

Inappropriate self-esteem

Incest

Infertility

Injustice

Job loss

Job stress

Lies

Loneliness

Loss

Marital conflict

Migraines

Molestation

Natural disasters

Obsessiveness

Pessimism

Quarrels

Racism

Rape

Rejection

Relational conflict

Self-inflicted sin

Separation

Slander

Splinter

Taunting

Temper

Temptation

Terrorism

Tragedy

Transgression

Unemployment

Unfaithfulness

Unfulfilling job

Unplanned pregnancy

Uselessness

Victimization

Vulnerability

Weariness

Widowhood

Worry

Yesterday's news

Yes, a few of these appear to be a lot less troubling than others, but in the moment, they can be just as stressful.

When we stay soaked in pain, it affects us mentally, emotionally, physically, relationally, and spiritually:

- Mentally—we experience cloudy decision-making, irrational thinking, warped memories, and anxiety.
- Emotionally—we are depressed, sad, full of despair, and frustrated; we want to be alone and feel worthless; self-esteem also takes a big hit.
- Physically—we are stressed, which can cause headaches, chronic pain, weight gain or loss, heart problems, stomach issues, and fatigue.

- Relationally—we seek revenge, want to retaliate, feel jealous, and compare ourselves to others; families split apart, and we don't allow others to get close.
- Spiritually—our relationship with God wanes as worship and prayer life ceases or slows; Scripture reading stops, and we separate ourselves from a community of believers.

I choose to hold on to the entire verse that Jesus spoke to his disciples: "I have told you these things, so that in me you may have peace. In this world you will have trouble. But take heart! I have overcome the world" (John 16:33).

When feeling helpless and drowning in pain, we need to take the focus from ourselves—the suffering, grief, problems, despair, hopelessness, helplessness—and shift it to Jesus. We can choose Jesus alone and find beautiful peace and hope in him.

Ripples

What troubles have come your way?

Past:

Present:

Make the choice to live out the following:

- Cry out: "Keep me safe, my God, for in you I take refuge" (Psalm 16:1).
- Pray: "Come near to God and he will come near to you" (James 4:8).

- Trust: "Trust in the Lord with all your heart and lean not on your own understanding" (Proverbs 3:5).

In the process of recording my first CD, *only HOPE in the storm*, my producer wanted to include songs that fit the theme of choosing Christ. He offered one that was uniquely his story.

Endless Tomorrows

Those precious drops that I thought were rain
Were really Your tears as You felt my pain
So much grief I couldn't bear it
So God became man and asked to share it

I'd like to believe those who say
"Just believing" makes it go away
But You ask me to follow You
Sometimes around and sometimes through

So enduring 'til the end
I won't break, but I will bend
Confident in my best friend
Trust God and not in man

In this world I will have troubles
In this life there will be sorrows
But one precious truth I cling to
There will be endless tomorrows
Through it all, you never leave me
Death is swallowed up in victory

No looking back until Your face I see
Throughout endless tomorrows
Endless tomorrows[2]

---

2.   "Endless Tomorrows," © 2005 Chet A. Chambers. Used by permission. Music and lyrics by Chet Chambers, performed by Debbie Roth on *only HOPE in the storm.*

Finding Peace in the Pain

You can't go back and make a new start, but you can start right now and make a brand-new ending.
                                        —James R. Sherman

B eing drenched in pain can leave us feeling crushed, alone, and without hope. Before we can heal, we have to figure out (with godly guidance) where, when, and how our troubles, struggles, and pain began.

In the summer of 1993, I was able to reach out to a Christian counselor, Charley Gerber, who took me from "drenched in pain" to "drenched in hope." We talked through painful past events, worked through distressful current events, studied Scripture, and prayed. Anger subsided, and finally, I believed I would get through—and leave behind—the agony of feeling worthless. I found my hope in Christ once again. Hope prevailed.

> Though I walk in the midst of trouble,
> you preserve my life.
> You stretch out your hand against the anger of my foes;
> with your right hand you save me.
> (Psalm 138:7)

Through experiences of my own, I have found pain to come in three ways:

- Pain caused by circumstances beyond our control, which may include death, disease, or natural disasters.
- Pain caused by the wrong choices of others, such as death due to an accident, abuse, rape, or betrayal.
- Pain caused by our own wrong choices, such as sin, giving into temptations, or making choices against God's will.

Pain Caused by Circumstances beyond Our Control

Why, God? Why do bad things happen? Why did my dad have to die of a terrible disease? Why have I had to struggle with breast cancer and severe osteoarthritis resulting in knee replacements? Why heart issues?

Each year at Christmas, my husband purchases a new ornament for us, representing the year. In 1998, he bought a fish holding a sign that said, "Holy Mackerel!" The ornament represented the very tough times we endured that year. In May, my husband resigned from his ministry position (leaving him without a job), my parents' fifty-year marriage ended in divorce, and five days later my father passed away from an eight-year battle with cancer. And that was just May.

In June, our oldest daughter graduated from high school. August found our family spreading my dad's ashes. In September, I cried as I looked in the rearview mirror leaving my daughter at college. When October came, I was diagnosed with breast cancer, followed by a double mastectomy in December to finish out the year. "Holy Mackerel!" indeed.

What a stinky year. (Side note: My dad loved to fish, which made the ornament even more appropriate.)

How I cried out to God in my soul. Why did Dad have to get cancer? Why couldn't he have been healed like I was? Why was it so hard to watch that first child graduate? Why wasn't my husband able to find a job for so long? Why was I diagnosed with breast cancer (leaving me with one choice— to get rid of it)? What did I do wrong, God?

"Why" questions run rampant when we struggle with events that cause deep-seated pain. Why do things like this happen? Why are people capable of wounding others so deeply? Why me? Why do I deserve this?

However, God often takes what others mean to harm us and uses it for our good. Let's look at a few examples from Scripture.

In the book of Job, we find an innocent man who honored God and stayed away from evil. He had seven sons and three daughters and a very comfortable life. God allowed Satan to test Job to prove he was loyal to God.

What happened to Job? All his animals were killed, as well as his children. Job's flesh and bones deteriorated, and friends wrongly accused him of sinning, saying all the troubles were his fault.

Did Job have "why" questions? Yes!

"Why did I not perish at birth?" (Job 3:11). "Why is light given to those in misery, and life to the bitter of soul, to those who long for death that does not come, who search for it more than for hidden treasure, who are filled with gladness and rejoice when they reach the grave?" (3:20–22). "Why have you made me your target? Have I become a burden to you?" (7:20). "Why do you hide your face and consider me your enemy?" (13:24).

Through all Job's questions, he did not sin or blame God. "Job replied to the LORD: 'I know that you can do all things; no plan of yours can be thwarted. . . . My ears had heard of you but now my eyes have seen you. Therefore I despise myself and repent in dust and ashes'" (42:1–2, 5–6).

After Job prayed for his friends, the Lord gave him twice as much as before. The Lord blessed the latter part of Job's life more than the first.

Job is not the only example of someone who suffered because of circumstances beyond his control, nor the only example of someone who handled it well. Gwen Griffin Arbuckle, a dear friend, posted on Facebook about the impact her differently-abled sister had on her:

> My sister, Pam, who was mentally handicapped, was also crippled and bedridden for many years before her passing. I was asked once who taught me the most about life … my answer was Pam. She loved everyone, no hate in her life, not even against those who made fun of her because she was "different." And she had a special love for her Savior; so much trust.

We can rarely answer the "why" questions when it comes to this kind of pain. We can only hold on to faith in God.

Pain Caused by the Wrong Choices of Others
As long as there are people living on this planet, wrong choices will cause pain in infinite ways:

Abuse	Lashing out in anger
Blatant lies	Searing words
Drunk driving	Sexual assault
Holding grudges	Subtle gossip
Infidelity	Theft

Rape is an ugly word, and "wrong choice" doesn't begin to convey the depth of anguish it brings. Not only was my physical virginity stolen from me, but it was stolen by someone I trusted. Perhaps that's what hurt the most. How could someone I knew and trusted do something like that to me?

It was horrible, to be sure, but it wasn't unique. I am one of many who have been betrayed by someone close to them.

In Genesis 37, we find the story of Joseph, the eleventh son of Jacob (Israel). There, we read, "Now Israel loved Joseph more than any of his other sons, because he had been born to him in his old age; and he made an ornate robe for him. When his brothers saw that their father loved him more than any of them, they hated him and could not speak a kind word to him" (Genesis 37:3–4).

That robe turned out to be more of a curse than a blessing. Look what happened next:

- His brothers hated him.
- They stole his robe.
- They threw him into a cistern.
- They sold him into slavery.
- They lied and told his father he was dead.
- Potiphar's wife accused him of a crime against her.
- Potiphar threw him into prison.
- The cupbearer, who was to put in a good word for him, forgot him.

(See Genesis 37–50 for the whole story.)

I would think all these things would have caused Joseph to become angry, wanting to retaliate. However, even though the wrong choices of others seemed to ruin his life, Joseph chose to keep his eyes on the Lord's way, and he received blessings in the midst of his troubles:

- As a slave, the Lord prospered Joseph, and he became a blessing to his owner's household.
- While in prison, the Lord showed him kindness and granted him favor in the eyes of the prison warden.
- Joseph received the gift of interpreting dreams.
- The chief cupbearer eventually remembered Joseph's ability to interpret dreams and recommended him to Pharaoh, who then brought him out of the dungeon.
- Pharaoh himself called Joseph "discerning and wise" and put him in charge of the whole land of Egypt. (Genesis 41:39)

The names of his children show Joseph's faith. Joseph named his firstborn Manasseh and said, "It is because God has made me forget all my trouble and all my father's household" (v. 51). The second son he named Ephraim and said, "It is because God has made me fruitful in the land of my suffering" (v. 52).

To his brothers, Joseph said, "You intended to harm me, but God intended it for good to accomplish what is now being done, the saving of many lives. So then, don't be afraid. I will provide for you and your children" (Genesis 50:20–21).

What an example of trusting God when others hurt and betray you! By God's grace, we can follow Joseph's example. It's difficult, but he will give you strength as you trust in him.

Someone made the horrible choice to kill Scarlett Lewis' child at Sandy Hook Elementary School. To lose a child that way would rattle the most devout Christian's faith, but Scarlett seemed to trust even in the midst of this most heart-wrenching storm. She said, "We can't always choose what happens to us, but we can always choose how we respond—and we can always respond with love."[3] This is the very heart of her Jesse Lewis Choose Love Movement.

Pain Caused by Our Own Wrong Choices

It might almost be comforting to think that our struggles are caused by circumstances out of our control or by the wrong choices of others, but that's not the whole picture. Sometimes our boat is taking on water because we drilled a hole in it! Max Lucado once wrote, "Where we might think of sin as slip-ups or missteps, God views sin as a godless attitude that leads to godless actions."[4] Even though God promises to forgive us, there are often negative consequences in this life when we sin. Have I ever given in to temptation? Am I guilty of envy? Have I been drunk with wine instead of being filled with the Spirit (Ephesians 5:18)? Absolutely, and it causes pain.

Instead, we are to "follow God's example, therefore, as dearly loved children and walk in the way of love, just as Christ loved us and gave himself up for us as a fragrant offering and sacrifice to God" (Ephesians 5:1–2).

---

3. Quoted at http://inspiring.ntd.tv/parenting/mom-of-sandy-hook-victim-finds-3-words-scribbled-by-her-son-which-changes-her-life-forever.html.
4. Max Lucado, "We're Made Whole," https://maxlucado.com/listen/were-made-whole/.

We are to be a fragrant offering, not full of stinky, selfish desires. What are some of these selfish desires? These are godless actions (to name a few) that appear in Scripture:

Adultery	Greed
Arguing	Hatred
Bitterness	Hypocrisy
Coarse joking	Idolatry
Complaining	Impurity
Debauchery	Malice
Deceitful desires	Murder
Discord	Obscenity
Disorder	Rage
Drunkenness	Selfish ambition
Envy	Sexual immorality
Evil thoughts	Slander
False testimony	Theft
Foolish talk	Unwholesome talk
Gossip	Witchcraft

I believe we get the idea. These behaviors reek before the Lord—and others notice.

Animals can carry an odor as well—not always pleasing. References to sheep are common in the Bible: flocks of sheep as possessions, sacrifice of sheep, sheep as nourishment, and sheep as a source of income.

Did Jesus ever spend time with stinky sheep? Consider Judas, Peter, the woman at the well, the leper, and Zacchaeus, to name just a few. Let's take a moment and look at the woman at the well. She was a Samaritan woman—Jewish men would not have given her the time of day. (They wouldn't have even traveled through Samaria but would've rerouted themselves to avoid "those people.") In fact, even other Samaritans made her an outcast because of her less-than-moral lifestyle. In other words, her behavior stunk. But Jesus spoke to her and offered her living water, unlike anything from an earthly well.

As Natalie Lloyd pointed out in her book, *Paperdoll*, Jesus didn't mind the Samaritan woman's mess. He was willing to step into it with her, to see her, to offer help and healing. Lloyd wrote, "We get to bring the whole entire mess of our heart to Jesus, just as it is. We get to sort out the pieces there in His presence. We get to take comfort in His love. . . . Yes, there are some deep places of pain in our hearts. But His love is deep enough to penetrate every last part."[5]

Have you noticed that your body picks up smells? Hang around a smoker, and you will smell like smoke. Sit around a campfire, and you will be airing out clothes or washing them. Receive a big hug from someone who loves perfume or cologne, and you will be wearing it the rest of the day.

The same happens if we hold on to the pain of our sins. We can end up carrying the odors of unforgiveness and anger—even bitterness. Unless we deal with our sin and ask God to cleanse us, we will always carry the stench.

But if we spend time with God, we'll wear the scent of him. We can ask him to help with forgiveness, with mercy and grace, with showing humility, compassion, and thankfulness. I choose to leave my life in his hands and allow his aroma to permeate me, thus becoming filled with "love, joy,

---

5. Natalie Lloyd, *Paperdoll* (Ventura, CA: Regal, 2009), 128.

peace, patience, kindness, goodness, faithfulness, gentleness, and self-control" (Galatians 5:22–23 NLT). We can leave sin's stench behind and become drenched in God's pleasing aroma.

There's a quote that has been attributed to so many different people that at this point it's impossible to tell who actually first said it, but it reminds us of the dangers of steeping in sin: "Sin will take you farther than you ever thought you'd go; it will keep you there longer than you ever intended to stay; and it will cost you more than you ever expected to pay."

We must remember we have a choice to make. We can isolate ourselves and wallow in the stench, or we can allow Jesus to wash us whiter than snow and surround ourselves with people who carry the aroma of Christ.

Ripples

Take a moment to categorize your struggles.

Pain caused by circumstances out of your control:

Pain caused by the wrong choices of others:

Pain caused by wrong choices of your own:

As you read these Scriptures, use them to help you pray about taking action:

- "Brothers and sisters, I do not consider myself yet to have taken hold of it. But one thing I do: Forgetting what is behind and straining toward what is ahead, I press on toward the goal to win the prize for which God has called me heavenward in Christ Jesus" (Philippians 3:13–14).
- "Cast all your anxiety on him because he cares for you" (1 Peter 5:7).
- "Come to me, all you who are weary and burdened, and I will give you rest. Take my yoke upon you and learn from me, for I am gentle and humble in heart, and you will find rest for your souls. For my yoke is easy and my burden is light" (Matthew 11:28–30).
- "No temptation has overtaken you except what is common to mankind. And God is faithful; he will not let you be tempted beyond what you can bear. But when you are tempted, he will also provide a way out so that you can endure it" (1 Corinthians 10:13).
- "If we confess our sins, he is faithful and just and will forgive us our sins and purify us from all unrighteousness" (1 John 1:9).

My second CD, *endless HOPE*, includes a song inspired by Robin Williams (no, not the comedian). Her poem captured the sense of being broken and hurting yet turning to the Prince of Peace.

Ragdoll

Lord, I come to you like a broken ragdoll
My dress is torn and stained
My arm is half hanging on
My eyes aren't shining and trusting
Like they once were
And my expression isn't innocent anymore

I'm not the unused, brand-new ragdoll I once was
Yes, my smile is still there
But not as bright as it once was
I'm a ragdoll
It's a little more forced now
A bit more tired
A broken ragdoll

I need to be picked up by you, Lord
Picked up held tightly loved and reassured
Reassured that no matter how I look
Or how dirty and scuffed up and broken I am
You love me just like I was brand-new
When I was brand-new

So I cried would you please hold me, Lord
He picked me up and held me close
And said you're not a broken ragdoll
You're my child
The child I chose[6]

---

6. "Ragdoll," © 2007 Chet A. Chambers. Used by permission. Music and lyrics by Chet Chambers, performed by Debbie Roth on *endless HOPE*.

Accepting God's Promises:
Only Hope in the Storm

A study of the life of eagles teaches that the eagle knows when a storm is coming and goes to a higher area to wait for the winds to actually lift it up above the storm. The eagle does not escape the storms, it simply uses them to take it higher. God enables us to do the same! It is not the burdens of life that weight us down, it is how we handle them. The eagle never gets weighted down.

—Alma Edith Welch

In 1978, I was trying to keep my head above water, feeling lost at sea, and caught up in the waves of a life I didn't want. I tried to distract myself from my pain with sex, alcohol, and marijuana. I had no concept of how the abuse of my upbringing led me there. Repressed emotions kept me floundering. And then, God provided a way to dry land. He sent me someone that became the only Jesus I had ever seen, a compassionate person who felt my pain. Over a few months, I saw beyond the deep waters to a hope I hadn't seen in a long time. The plan of walking with Jesus Christ forever was laid out before me, and I soon understood what this offering of love, comfort, peace, rest, and hope meant. I just needed to open my eyes, listen intently with my ears, unclench my fists, and lift my arms to accept God's promises.

In her book *When I Lay My Isaac Down*, Carol Kent said something that completely resonated with me: "Would I honor God by continuing to love and trust Him in these utterly unthinkable circumstances, or would I spend my days trying to direct an outcome that was so clearly beyond my control?"[7]

Sometimes we can feel the onset of a painful storm coming. Sometimes that storm takes us by surprise, and we find ourselves suddenly adrift and clinging to our raft, trying to keep it from capsizing so we aren't left to sink or swim.

Sometimes we ask, God, where are you? He's reaching out his hand to offer us a lifeline, to pull us in from the storm, just as Jesus reached out to Peter when he was frightened of the storm and sinking into the deep (Matthew 14:22–32).

God provides ways to protect us from drowning. There is hope, not only in our trials and tribulations but for our daily needs as well. He offers stabilizing compassion and comfort, forgiveness and peace, rest, love, and hope. And often, his promises lift us up, allowing us a new perspective to face adversity and a higher place to ride out the storms.

The first step is believing God, taking him at his word. Read the following verses, and ask God to help you trust the truths you find:

- "For God so loved the world that he gave his one and only Son, that whoever believes in him shall not perish but have eternal life" (John 3:16).

---

7.   Carol Kent, *When I Lay My Isaac Down* (Colorado Springs: NavPress, 2004), 42.

- "If you declare with your mouth, 'Jesus is Lord,' and believe in your heart that God raised him from the dead, you will be saved" (Romans 10:9).
- Jesus said, "I am the resurrection and the life. The one who believes in me will live, even though they die, and whoever lives by believing in me will never die" (John 11:25–26).
- "I have come into the world as a light, so that no one who believes in me should stay in darkness" (John 12:46).

The next step is surrendering our circumstances and expectations to God and trusting in the only one who is always trustworthy:

- "When you pass through the waters, I will be with you; and when you pass through the rivers, they will not sweep over you. When you walk through the fire, you will not be burned; the flames will not set you ablaze" (Isaiah 43:2).
- "Those who know your name will trust in you, for you, LORD, have never forsaken those who seek you" (Psalm 9:10).
- "LORD Almighty, blessed is the one who trusts in you" (Psalm 84:12).
- "Don't let your hearts be troubled. Trust in God, and trust also in me" (John 14:1 NLT).
- "Peace I leave with you; my peace I give you. I do not give to you as the world gives. Do not let your hearts be troubled and do not be afraid" (John 14:27).

As we practice the first two steps consistently, we are able to accept and fully receive the benefit of his promises:

Comfort	Kindness
Compassion	Love
Faithfulness	Mercy
Forgiveness	Patience
Grace	Peace
His presence with us	Rest
Hope	Strength

Dan Roelofs, a young pastor from Minnesota, understood surrender. In order to truly be yielded to God, we must let go of our need to control our circumstances. Surrender can even require that we turn our expectations loose and simply accept God's plan for us. I think this is why Dan Roelofs' testimony is so striking. Dan died on his thirty-third birthday, March 20, 2003, but the life he lived up to that point was one of belief, surrender, trust, and acceptance. Cancer may have claimed his body, but Jesus had the ultimate claim on his soul. A quote from Roelofs' book, *A Place Called Surrender*, is written on his gravestone:

> We are assured of God's love and know that our only rest is in surrender. He is asking us to lay down everything that we would cling to in order that we can embrace Him, even if that means my life. In the end we will know Him more intimately, trust Him absolutely, and obey Him more faithfully. His love truly is better than life![8]

8.   Dan Roelofs, *A Place Called Surrender* (Elk River, MN: One Passion Publishing, 2002), 117.

King David also understood that accepting God's promises leads to a life filled with peace, protection, and joy.

But let all who take refuge in you be glad;
    let them ever sing for joy.
Spread your protection over them,
    that those who love your name may rejoice in you.
(Psalm 5:11)

Ripples

As you read these promises, insert your name in the blanks and accept the promises as your own.

- "Cast all your anxiety on him because he cares for you, _____" (1 Peter 5:7).
- "Come to me, _____, you who are weary and burdened, and I will give you rest. Take my yoke upon you and learn from me, for I am gentle and humble in heart, and, _____, you will find rest for your soul. For My yoke is easy and my burden is light" (Matthew 11:28–30).

- "Be alert, _____, and of sober mind. Your enemy the devil prowls around like a roaring lion looking for someone to devour. Resist him, _____, standing firm in the faith, because you know that the family of believers throughout the world is undergoing the same kind of sufferings. And the God of all grace, who called you, _____, to his eternal glory in Christ, after you, _____, have suffered a little while, will himself restore you and make you strong, firm and steadfast" (1 Peter 5:8–10).

- "[I] can rejoice, too, when [I] run into problems and trials, for [I] know that they help (me) develop endurance. And endurance develops strength of character, and character strengthens (my) confident hope of salvation. And this hope will not lead to disappointment. For [I] know how dearly God loves (me), because he has given (me) the Holy Spirit to fill (my) heart with his love" (Romans 5:3–5 NLT).

Do you not know? Have you not heard? The LORD is the everlasting God, the Creator of the ends of the earth. He will not grow tired or weary, and his understanding no one can fathom. He gives strength to the weary and increases the power of the weak. Even youths grow tired and weary, and young men stumble and fall; but those who hope in the LORD will renew their strength. They will soar on wings like eagles; they will run and not grow weary, they will walk and not be faint. (Isaiah 40:28–31)

This classic hymn with additional lyrics by my producer, Chet Chambers, can be anyone's anthem.

It Is Well with My Soul

When peace like a river attendeth my way
When sorrows like sea billows roll
Whatever my lot, Thou hast taught me to say
It is well, it is well with my soul

Though Satan should buffet, though trials should come
Let this blest assurance control
That Christ has regarded my helpless estate
And hath shed His own blood for my soul

It is well
With my soul
It is well, it is well with my soul

It is well, it is well
Even when I'm tossed about
By storms sent straight from the depths of hell
My Savior pulls me out
Through the wind and the waves
Hear me shout, "my Jesus saves!"
Praise the Lord, it is well with my soul

My sin—o the bliss of this glorious thought
My sin—not in part, but the whole
Is nailed to the cross, and I bear it no more
Praise the Lord, praise the Lord, o my soul
And Lord haste the day when my faith shall be sight
The clouds be rolled back as a scroll
The trump shall resound and the Lord shall descend
Even so, it is well with my soul
It is well
With my soul
It is well, it is well with my soul[9]

Yes, we are drenched in struggles, but we can stand in the storm!

---

9.   "It Is Well with My Soul," Additional lyric © 2005 Chet A. Chambers. Used by permission. Written by Horatio G. Spafford/Philip P. Bliss (Public Domain), performed by Debbie Roth on *only HOPE in the storm*.

Singing in the Rain: Drenched in Survival

Edy and her husband, Harold, were the bright spots in my early childhood. When the first two houses in the neighborhood were built, my parents bought one, and Edy and Harold moved in next door. Until I was eight, we joined each other for holiday dinners, alternating houses for Thanksgiving and Christmas. Pictures showed two happy families, enjoying being together.

When I was four, I ran into our garage and was going to head into the house through the back door. Unfortunately, the door didn't open, and my hand crashed through, shattering glass everywhere. Terrified, I yanked my arm back and sliced it on the jagged edge of the broken shards. That fearful reaction severed the artery in my wrist. If we would have gotten to the hospital even a few minutes later, I would not be sitting here today writing this book. I don't remember much after that besides my dad rushing to the door of the house with a towel wrapped around his neck—he'd been in the middle of washing his hair.

Someone later told me my mom's main concern about my accident was that it was interrupting her dinner preparations.

But Edy knew I'd need comfort and attention. She's the one who sat in the backseat of the car with me as Dad drove us to the hospital. She, a nurse, held my arm so tightly it was incredibly painful, but having her there calmed me, despite the pain. She cuddled me, wiped my tears, and spoke gently to me.

I don't know what Mom was doing during that time, but if she'd come, I can't imagine her being such a comfort. She never did any of the things Mother's Day cards described.

But I had Edy, and at the time, that was enough.

She's the one who played with me, laughing at every little thing. She loved to play the piano and would let me sit on her lap as she played. She took me on outings to rockhound gatherings, and I was even the flower girl in her son's wedding. I still have the golden dress I wore. She was a mom to me. What a gift from God!

My heart longed to be with this "mom." I knew she loved me and wanted to spend time with me. With her, I found the happiness to ease the pain inflicted within the walls of my own home. I believe through sweet Edy's unselfish kindness God granted me an opportunity to sing in the rain, even though drenched in struggles. My mom neglected me, but with Edy's love, I could continue singing.

4

Perseverance

When you get into a tight place and everything goes against you, till it seems as though you could not hold on a minute longer, never give up then, for that is just the place and time that the tide will turn.

—Harriet Beecher Stowe

The drenching storm constantly taps on the umbrella, reminding you the rain is not over yet. Your cold, numb feet slosh through the water that hurriedly flows to the drains. You aren't sure how you made it this far. *Will I have the strength to keep going?* you wonder. All you want is to reach your destination and dry off, so your aching feet continue on a journey of perseverance—toward survival.

Following two knee replacements and an Achilles tendon repair, I needed to get back to my preferred method of exercise: walking. I started down a path I had enjoyed many times and soon met a gentleman from our church traveling the opposite way. I commented that he seemed to be a long way from home. He said it wasn't so bad because the path continued behind his home.

"Really? I thought it stopped at the T."

"No," he replied, explaining that it kept going much farther than I'd known.

Excited to discover a new path, I set out to walk the entire length of the path the next day. However, I soon came upon an unexpected stop sign, and from there, I couldn't tell where the path continued. Upon returning home, I checked a map. A rise on the edge of the road had hidden the way.

On my next walk, I pressed on, exploring farther. Oh, what a sight! Lilies, dahlias, and daisies bloomed in gorgeous landscaped yards; ducks sang in their own language as they floated through the creek. I could have given up when the path became obscured and lost my chance to see all that beauty. Had I not believed my friend's directions and had I lacked the determination to find the rest of the path, I would have missed so much of what God wanted me to experience.

Singing in the rain starts with moving beyond the stop signs that hinder our healing. Stop signs come in many forms, but all of them would limit us from experiencing all that God offers us. In my own life, I've seen stop signs in the forms of anger, unforgiveness, fear, worry about what is coming next, and mistrust that God could calm my storm. When you come to stop signs in your journey, how can you convince yourself to move forward and see the reward on the other side of the obstacles?

Yes, rewards wait for those who persevere. "Blessed is the one who perseveres under trial because, having stood the test, that person will receive the crown of life that the Lord has promised to those who love him" (James 1:12).

Perseverance is not just gritting our teeth. Perseverance involves action. In chapter 3, we looked at what God offers as lifelines to protect us from drowning, allowing us to face adversity head on with hope:

- Believing God and taking him at his word
- Surrendering our circumstances and expectations to God and trusting him with the results
- Accepting and fully receiving the benefit of his promises

Now, let's consider some things that oppose that guidance and protection.

Anger and Bitterness

In order to continue on (like extending the length of my walks), persevere, and find the hope God promises, a couple significant stop signs need our attention: anger and bitterness. Ephesians 4:31–32 addresses and offers direction for both of these hurting-heart emotions: "Get rid of all bitterness, rage and anger, brawling and slander, along with every form of malice. Be kind and compassionate to one another, forgiving each other, just as in Christ God forgave you."

Anger toward God

Our anger brings out questions like "Why?" and "How could you let this happen?" and "Don't you love me?" When pain is caused by circumstances beyond our control, it is a natural reaction to want to assign blame. Death, natural disasters, and disease have no outlet for blame, no one to hold responsible, so we cry out to God with our anger-fueled inquiries.

It is natural to want answers, and it's encouraging to see biblical examples that show we aren't alone in our questioning:

- Job's anger—"I cry out to you, God, but you do not answer; I stand up, but you merely look at me. You turn on me ruthlessly; with the might of your hand you attack me. You snatch me up and drive me before the wind; you toss me about in the storm" (Job 30:20–22).
- David's anger—"My God, my God, why have you forsaken me? Why are you so far from saving me, so far from my cries of anguish? My God, I cry out by day, but you do not answer, by night, but I find no rest" (Psalm 22:1–2).

Of course, if we stop here and don't persevere through the anger, then our story will have a disappointing ending, much like Jonah's. My thanks to my husband for the following summary of Jonah's story:

God had a job for Jonah to do. He wanted Jonah to go to Nineveh and preach. Jonah immediately packed up a few of his things and headed off in a boat . . . in the opposite direction!

God sent a storm, and Jonah knew it was his fault. Jonah also knew the only way to silence the raging winds was for the sailors to throw him overboard. So they did.

And the storm stopped.

But there was Jonah, in the middle of the Mediterranean, trying to stay afloat without a boat. God sent an unexpected rescuer: a large fish showed up and swallowed Jonah down.

After three days and nights, God commanded the fish to spit Jonah onto the shore.

God still had a job for Jonah to do, and this time, Jonah knew better than to say no to God. So Jonah walked through the streets of Nineveh (which was such a big city, it took three days!) preaching, "Forty more days, and Nineveh will be overthrown!" Then Jonah went outside the city and waited to see what would happen.

Well, the people of Nineveh, from the street vendors to the king himself, all repented of their evil ways and cried out to God for mercy, who, as always, was happy to give it.

You would think Jonah would be glad his preaching had such a positive effect.

And you would be wrong.

In fact, Jonah was angry. You see, Nineveh was an enemy of Israel. Jonah didn't want God to show mercy to them. Besides, Jonah had preached that Nineveh would be overthrown, and now it wasn't being overthrown, and that made Jonah look stupid . . . if not worse.

While Jonah sat and fumed, God had one more lesson to teach him. He caused a leafy plant to quickly grow beside Jonah, shading him from the piercing sun. That made Jonah happy. Then, just as quickly, God made the plant wither away. No more shade for Jonah. That made Jonah angry.

And here's the lesson, straight from the mouth of God: "You have been concerned about this plant, though you did not tend it or make it grow. It sprang up overnight and died overnight. Should I not have concern for the great city of Nineveh, in which there are more than a hundred twenty thousand people who cannot tell their right hand from their left?" (Jonah 4:10–11).[10]

In other words, "Jonah, there's a whole lot more going on in the world than what you see as being personally important to you." Maybe, just maybe, if a person finds themselves angry at God, it could be because they aren't on board with God's plans.

Anger toward the Person Causing Our Pain

When we have been hurt or violated by someone, it is so easy to want to cause them pain like we've experienced. "How could they do that to me? I want something bad to happen to them, so they experience this pain!"

David expressed this kind of anger well in Psalm 3:7: "Arise, Lord! Deliver me, my God! Strike all my enemies on the jaw; break the teeth of the wicked."

Or as singer/songwriter Rich Mullins said at least once, "I know vengeance is mine, thus saith the Lord, but I just want to be about the Lord's business."[11]

Obviously, these reactions are a common part of being human. They are normal. They just aren't helpful.

Anger toward Ourselves

"I can't believe I did that! I'm so stupid! I'm not good enough. How could God ever love me? I deserve what happened to

---

10. Dewey Roth, in discussion with the author, January 2018. Used by permission.
11. Rich Mullins, Footage from a concert in Lufkin, Texas, https://youtu.be/vQnFU5JvuWY.

mc." These lies convince us we're not worthy of anything more, and we want to dull the pain with drugs or alcohol. We want to fill the void with food or control every single calorie we take in, so we can be different. We want to feel something, *anything* else, so we harm ourselves. Or oddly enough, we turn our negative self-esteem into an inappropriate pride, often lashing out and inflicting pain on others.

Bitterness

Anger cries out to God in frustration. Bitterness is anger buried inside and allowed to fester. What does bitterness look like? It pushes us away from God.

Charley Gerber, in his book *Healing for a Bitter Heart*, offers these observations:

- In Psalm 73:21–22, David wrote, "When my heart was grieved and my spirit embittered, I was senseless and ignorant; I was a brute beast before you." Bitter people frequently do "senseless acts of violence" against others.
- In Acts 8:23 Peter is quoted as saying to Simon, "For I see that you are full of bitterness and captive to sin." Bitterness can become so consuming that it can be seen on the outside appearance of a person.
- Hebrews 12:15 reminds us, "See to it that no one misses the grace of God and that no bitter root grows up to cause trouble and defile many." The root of bitterness entangles itself around every aspect of a person's life. And it spreads. The taller your bitterness grows, the deeper and wider its root system reaches, and the more it undermines.

- Proverbs 14:10 says, "Each heart knows its own bitterness, and no one can share its joy." One of the reasons why a bitter person has no joy is because bitterness squeezes out the feelings of the presence of God.[12]

The Bible contains many Scriptures to help you persevere through anger and bitterness to find hope and joy. The following are just a few:
- "He heals the brokenhearted and binds up their wounds" (Psalm 147:3).
- "My dear brothers and sisters, take note of this: Everyone should be quick to listen, slow to speak and slow to become angry, because human anger does not produce the righteousness that God desires" (James 1:19–20).
- "Be joyful in hope, patient in affliction, faithful in prayer. . . .If it is possible, as far as it depends on you, live at peace with everyone. . . . Do not be overcome by evil, but overcome evil with good" (Romans 12:12, 18, 21).
- "Finally brothers and sisters, whatever is true, whatever is noble, whatever is right, whatever is pure, whatever is lovely, whatever is admirable—if anything is excellent or praiseworthy—think about such things" (Philippians 4:8).

---

12. Charles R. Gerber, *Healing for a Bitter Heart* (Joplin, MO: College Press, 1996), 50–53.

The Perseverance of Paul

Paul is a great example in Scripture of someone who persevered, regardless of the trials and tribulations he experienced. In fact, Paul wrote many of the words on perseverance and pressing on that we just read.

What storms did Paul endure?

- Imprisonment
- Floggings
- Exposure to death again and again
- Thirty-nine lashes (times five)
- A beating with rods (times three)
- Stoning
- A shipwreck
- Danger from rivers, bandits, Gentiles, his own countrymen, and false brothers (in the city and country and at sea)
- Labor and toil
- Exhaustion and lack of sleep
- Hunger and thirst, often living without food
- Cold and nakedness

(See 2 Corinthians 11:23–27 to read Paul's own account.)

In spite of all that, Paul was still able to pass on these words of encouragement:

- "May the God who gives endurance and encouragement give you the same attitude of mind toward each other that Christ Jesus had, so that with one mind and one voice you may glorify the God and Father of our Lord Jesus Christ" (Romans 15:5–6).
- "May the God of hope fill you with all joy and peace as you trust in him, so that you may overflow with

hope by the power of the Holy Spirit" (Romans 15:13).

- "He will also keep you firm to the end, so that you will be blameless on the day of our Lord Jesus Christ. God is faithful, who has called you into fellowship with his Son, Jesus Christ our Lord" (1 Corinthians 1:8–9).
- "But we have this treasure in jars of clay to show that this all-surpassing power is from God and not from us. We are hard pressed on every side, but not crushed; perplexed, but not in despair; persecuted, but not abandoned; struck down, but not destroyed" (2 Corinthians 4:7–9).
- "That is why, for Christ's sake, I delight in weaknesses, in insults, in hardships, in persecutions, in difficulties. For when I am weak, then I am strong" (2 Corinthians 12:10).
- "Not that I have already obtained all this, or have already arrived at my goal, but I press on to take hold of that for which Christ Jesus took hold of me" (Philippians 3:12).

Ripples

Sit quietly and consider the following words as aspects of perseverance for you to grow stronger in:

A–Z of Perseverance

Assurance/Ambition/
  Attitude
Belief
Confidence/
  Commitment/Courage
Determination/
  Diligence/Devotion
Endurance
Faithfulness
Growth/Grit/Grace
Hope/Humility
Imagination
Justification
Knowledge
Longing
Mindfulness/Mettle/
  Moxie

Nerve
Overcoming
Pressing On/Persistence/
  Patience/Passion
Quietness
Renewal/Restoration
Seeking/Steadfastness/
  Standing firm
Thirst/Transformation
Undivided/Unfading/
  Unfailing
Value/Vigor
Willingness/
  Wholeheartedness
X-pectation
Yearning
Zeal

> Not that I have already obtained all this, or have already been made perfect, but I press on to take hold of that for which Christ Jesus took hold of me. Brothers and sisters, I do not consider myself yet to have taken hold of it. But one thing I do: Forgetting what is behind and straining toward what is ahead, I press on toward the goal to win the prize for which God has called me heavenward in Christ Jesus. (Philippians 3:12–14)

For my second CD, I asked my husband to write a song that captured the idea of persevering through a storm and the empowerment only God can provide.

Captain of My Soul

Sometimes the seas of my life are all glassy
Peaceful and calm as a morning in spring
But it seems that more often my boat is in turmoil
In need of the comfort
That you alone can bring

Hurricanes turn to the breath of Your Spirit
Filling my canvas and helping me sail
But the journey's not easy and the waves come a-crashing
With You at the helm
I know I cannot fail

You blow me away
Away to the coming of day
The storm waves goodbye
As You burst through the sky
Your breath fills my sails
Empowering me as You blow me away
Captain of my soul,
Blow me away

It's not that You said you would stop the storms raging
Or hush the wind's howling that tempts me to fear
It's just that You promised to be with me always
Oh Jesus my Captain,
I'm glad that You are here

I'd never wish that strong storms would assail me
And yet, without fail, the trials inspire

You promise to always work things out for good
Whenever I'm sinking
Your grace lifts me higher and higher[13]

---

13. "Captain of My Soul," © 2007 Music GGGGus, Chet A. Chambers. Used by permission. Words and Music by Dewey Roth & Chet Chambers, performed by Debbie Roth on *endless HOPE.*

5

Forgiveness

In the shadow of my hurt, forgiveness feels like a decision to reward my enemy. But in the shadow of the cross, forgiveness is merely a gift from one undeserving soul to another.

—Andy Stanley

Being drenched in determination to survive not only entails persevering through the pain and dealing with anger and bitterness but understanding how we are to forgive others and ourselves just as God forgave us. Though what follows may seem like a long story, it is one way I was able to survive a storm in my life.

In the first week of February 2004, I received a phone call from my brother. My mom wasn't expected to live much longer. On February 4, I learned that she had passed in the nursing home, lying on a mattress on the floor. (You see, she kept falling out of bed, and because of restraint laws, the nursing home decided to put her on the floor.)

When I received the news of her death, I was a confused ball of emotions: sadness at her death, anger because I wished I could have had a nice mom, relief that our family was released from all the pain she had caused, regret because I wondered if I could have cared for her better.

Though I turned down having Mom tested for Alzheimer's, the doctor was sure that was her diagnosis, along with several other health issues. Signs began a few years prior, and I'd promised my dad (who was struggling with cancer) I would make sure Mom was taken care of. There I was, 900 miles away, trying to provide for the needs of a woman who had alienated everyone close to her.

My mom's meanness did not become obvious to me until I was in my teens. She was very controlling, manipulative, uncaring, and at times just didn't make sense. She showed no love, other than an overabundance of gifts at birthday celebrations and Christmases. When I received awards for my business studies or singing, she didn't rejoice with me. I don't know if she ever attended any choir concerts, though she may have been there. Every Saturday morning, I scrubbed the toilets and dusted, two jobs she always proceeded to redo. She never took me shopping for school clothes. In fact, the only time I remember going to a store with her was when I requested she come with me to pick out my wedding dress.

Soon after my engagement and the forced shopping trip, my parents and brother moved from Indiana where I was born back to Wyoming, where Mom was from and where my parents' married life had begun. Almost every summer, my husband and I packed up our growing family and made the trek to Wyoming for a visit.

After fifty years of marriage, Mom and Dad divorced, and Mom's signs of dementia became more and more apparent.

Eventually, the doctor made the decision to move her to a nursing home, a place she would never leave.

When the call came telling me of her death, I arranged a flight. From the airport, I was driven straight to the funeral home. There, I found my grandma (Mom's mother) and my step-grandfather distraught and in tears. They soon left, as well as my brother, and I was alone in the funeral home, with an open casket, for two and a half hours. I knew no one would show up to pay condolences, that there would be no flowers delivered from anyone. Just my deceased mom and me.

As I stood over her, the same feelings washed over me—sadness, anger, relief, release, regret. I knew if the lid of that casket closed without forgiveness taking place regret would rain over me. So, Mom and I had a long talk (okay, I did all the talking). I let her know how much she hurt me and asked why she couldn't be the mom the Mother's Day cards talked about. I felt sorry for her because she had missed out on so much happiness. Regrets? Sure, I wished things could have been said before the onset of her dementia; however, she became even more mean-spirited through the illness. Before the casket closed, I forgave her for all the heartache she had caused me and prayed that she somehow found peace with God before she passed.

The only way I could know how to forgive her was by understanding what God did for me. He loved me so much that he died on a cross for me, even knowing what a sinful wreck I would be. He saw what I could be, and he loved me like that.

Entire books have been written about forgiveness, and you'll find some recommendations in the back of this book, but for now, let's consider these three focal points:

- Asking God for forgiveness
- Forgiving the person who caused your pain
- Forgiving yourself

Asking God for Forgiveness

During that production of *Godspell* back in 1978, I realized I needed someone who would love me unconditionally, provide compassion, comfort, understanding, and peace, and offer hope—eternal hope. Feeling torn down, used up, and worthless, on May 25, 1978, I gave everything to the Lord, confessed my sins, asked for forgiveness, was washed as white as snow (Isaiah 1:18), and began a new life in Christ. I knew finally I'd found someone who would walk with me. With unconditional love, God wrapped his arms around me and promised he always would, even when storms came. Best of all? He promised eternal life through Jesus Christ.

In Scripture, God lays down clear milestones in our journey with him, so we can be sure we have his forgiveness:

- Understand all have sinned (Romans 3:23; 5:12).
- Acknowledge that "the wages of sin is death, but the gift of God is eternal life" (Romans 6:23; John 3:16, 18).
- Believe (Acts 16:30–31).
- Repent (Acts 16:30–31).
- Confess (Romans 10:9–10; 1 John 1:9).
- Be baptized (Acts 2:38; Mark 16:16; Matthew 3:13–15).
- Remain faithful (Revelation 2:10, 26).

Forgiving the Person Who Caused Your Pain

Scripture taught me I needed to forgive others as Christ forgave me (Ephesians 4:32). I never knew how God's forgiveness would give me strength until I needed to forgive those who would never say they were sorry for their wrongdoing. At a ladies' retreat where I spoke, someone asked how I knew I had actually forgiven the people who caused me so much pain. My answer? I knew I'd forgiven them when I realized I wasn't angry at them anymore, just sad that those situations happened. I knew I had forgiven them when I could pray for them. When I was able to pray for my rapists, abusers, and betrayers and forgive them the way the Lord had forgiven me, I knew the peace I experienced was a direct gift from God.

I have been betrayed more than once in my life. Betrayal has come through lying, gloating, deceit, misconstrued stories, and harsh judgment. It's easy to head in the direction of bitterness, but when God's grace puts healing salve and bandages on those wounds, he makes a person able to forgive and heal. Forgiveness isn't a switch you can flip. It is a process.

Many people resist forgiveness because it feels like they are condoning the offender's actions. It isn't. And it doesn't necessarily "make friends" or give the person an opportunity to offend again either. What it does is put the situation in God's hands and allow *you* to move forward in healing.

These Scriptures deepened my understanding of forgiveness:

- "Bear with each other and forgive one another if any of you has a grievance against someone. Forgive as the Lord forgave you" (Colossians 3:13).
- "And when you stand praying, if you hold anything against anyone, forgive them, so that your Father in heaven may forgive you your sins" (Mark 11:25).
- "You have heard that it was said, 'Love your neighbor and hate your enemy.' But I tell you, love your enemies and pray for those who persecute you" (Matthew 5:43–44).
- "Do not repay anyone evil for evil. Be careful to do what is right in the eyes of everybody. If it is possible, as far as it depends on you, live at peace with everyone. Do not take revenge, my dear friends, but leave room for God's wrath, for it is written: 'It is mine to avenge; I will repay,' says the Lord" (Romans 12:17–19).

Forgiving Yourself (The Hardest Person to Forgive)

It's easy to see our need to forgive ourselves when our own wrong decisions cause our struggles. But even when others' wrong choices cause our pain, we can sometimes be overcome by guilt and shame: Was I in the wrong place at the wrong time? Maybe if I just numb the pain with drugs and alcohol . . . Why doesn't my mom like me, and why did she say she wished I'd never been born? Maybe if I strive to be perfect, she would love me. Why can't I be good enough? Why does temptation have such a firm grasp that it entangles me in sin? If I wouldn't have given in . . .

When we refuse to forgive ourselves, we are setting ourselves up as having more authority than the loving heavenly Father who has forgiven us. He wants us to feel loved; who are we to say no to that? Why would we turn our backs on the hope, joy, and peace the Bible talks about?

- "Don't let your hearts be troubled. Trust in God, and trust also in me" (John 14:1 NLT).
- "Peace I leave with you; my peace I give you. I do not give to you as the world gives. Do not let your hearts be troubled and do not be afraid" (John 14:27).
- "May the God of hope fill you with all joy and peace as you trust in him, so that you may overflow with hope by the power of the Holy Spirit" (Romans 15:13).

Forgiveness is freeing. It is surrendering to God, the one who loves you so much he died for you. He forgave us, and when we forgive ourselves and others, we receive the promise of hope and peace.

God keeps working on us and stays with us all through our journey. In Philippians 1:6, Paul says, "And I am certain that God, who began the good work within you, will continue his work until it is finally finished on the day when Christ Jesus returns" (NLT).

Ripples

Three simple prayers for your consideration:

- For forgiveness from God: *Lord, you are always right, and I have been wrong so often. Forgive me and change my heart.*

- For forgiving others: *Give me a heart like yours, Father. Help me forgive those who have wronged me, just like you have forgiven me. Even if they don't want or feel the need for my forgiveness, help me to let go of the pain and indignation. Help me to give those things to you, so I can be free. This is a burden I don't want to carry any longer.*
- In thankfulness: *Thank you, God, for loving me so well and giving me hope.*

The idea of being a continuing project of God's handiwork is what I sang about in this song from my second CD, written by my producer and inspired by Psalm 66:10, "For you, God, tested us; you refined us like silver."

As Silver Refined

Remember when things get tough
God sees you as a diamond in the rough
Or like the potter sees the clay
Or the silversmith who takes the dross away
While you're going through the times of testing
Just remember this one thing
The hand that's shaping you
Has been pierced right through

As silver refined
As gold in the fire
He purifies me for a purpose much higher

Melting and molding and shaping my soul
Purging sin and making me whole
As silver refined
He makes me shine
'Till others can see his heart reflect in mine
Jesus let me shine like silver refined
Like gold in the fire

It's hard to forget the troubles
Tough to see past the pain
But Jesus can sympathize
He's been there too
And He's right there for you
So keeping our grip on hope
When it seems you're at the end
And you just can't cope
The hand that's shaping you
Has been pierced right through

The fire cleanses and purifies
Your heart begins to live
The moment that it dies[14]

---

14. "As Silver Refined," © 2007 Chet A. Chambers. Used by permission.
Words and Music by Chet Chambers, performed by Debbie Roth on *endless HOPE.*

Clothed in God's Grace: Endless Hope

Grace is not blind. It sees the hurt full well. But grace chooses to see God's forgiveness even more. It refuses to let hurts poison the heart. "See to it that no one misses the grace of God and that no bitter root grows up to cause trouble and defile many"(Hebrews 12:15). Where grace is lacking, bitterness abounds. Where grace abounds, forgiveness grows.

—Max Lucado

Looking for love in all the wrong places. Yes, that was me! After being raped at twelve, I believed defeating lies about myself. See, I knew the two young men who raped me. It actually took many years before I was able to admit that I was "maybe" raped. Convinced that I was in the wrong place at the wrong time, I always thought "maybe" the violation was my fault or "maybe" they just really liked me. As a result, desperate for comfort and love, I filled my preteen and teen years with promiscuous behaviors. Unfortunately, these pursuits led me to numb the torrential feelings with drugs and alcohol.

I met Jesus Christ at nineteen and found the very compassion, comfort, and love I so craved. Life continued on with marriage and family; however, labeling that first sexual event as rape never occurred to me until I attended workshops about date rape at Christ In Youth conferences. I was drawn to what the workshop leader, Charley Gerber (who later became my Christian counselor), had to say about date rape. When I finally dealt with past and present pain, I realized rape was, indeed, what happened.

I share this piece of my timeline with you to continue talking about the grace, mercy, and comfort that God lavished on me. Using Paul's words in Acts 20:22, 24, "And now, compelled by the Spirit . . . I consider my life worth nothing to me; my only aim is to finish the race and complete the task the Lord Jesus has given me—the task of testifying to the good news of God's grace."

What Is the Good News of God's Grace?

It's the absolutely true account of Jesus choosing to love me, not because I'm lovable but because he is love. It's the complete story of him taking my cross, bearing the punishment for my sin, and laying down his life for me.

It's the story one woman could tell about when she met Jesus face to face. You can find her story in chapter 8 of John's gospel. Once again, I've asked my husband to tell the tale as briefly as possible:

> Jesus was teaching in the temple when a group of religious leaders, jealous of Jesus' popularity, brought a woman who had been caught in the act of adultery and threw her at his feet.

"The law of Moses says we should stone this woman to death. What do you say, Jesus?"

Don't bother asking where the male half of the cheating couple was. Scripture doesn't say. The Pharisees weren't there to punish sin, anyway. They wanted to trap Jesus into either denying the Law by telling them to set the woman free or by advocating capital punishment, which the Roman occupying forces had reserved as only their privilege.

The bottom line is, Jesus didn't do either of the two things they expected.

"He who is without sin, cast the first stone."

That's all it took to take the wind out of the Pharisees' sails. They dropped their rocks and slipped away.

Jesus turned to the frightened, ashamed woman and asked, "Where are they? Has no one condemned you?"

"No one, Lord."

And now, here's where the grace comes in.

Can you see the softness in Jesus' face as He looked the woman in the eyes and said, "Neither do I condemn you; go, and from now on sin no more."[15]

Jesus didn't ignore the fact that she was an adulterer. He called sin *sin*, but he refused to let that be the end of the story. In the words of Timothy Keller, "God sees us as we are . . . but by His grace, He does not leave us as we are."[16]

---

15. Dewey Roth, in discussion with the author, January 2018. Used by permission.
16. Tweeted by @timkellernyc on May 16, 2014, twitter.com/timkellernyc.

That's good news we don't want to miss out on. "See to it that no one falls short of the grace of God" (Hebrews 12:15).

What do we look like if we miss the free gift of grace?

If our pain is caused by circumstances beyond our control, we could remain in anger, selfishness, jealousy, anxiety, and hopelessness. Our furrowed brows will deepen, the light in our eyes will darken, and our bodies will bear the burden of our troubled hearts.

If our pain is caused by the wrong choices of others, we could remain in bitterness, wanting revenge, and full of unforgiveness, hate, and fear. We will be weighed down by the anger we're holding on to and unable to live in the light of a peaceful spirit.

If our own wrong choices or sins are causing our pain, our total demeanor will be drenched in guilt, shame, worldly passion, disrespect, inappropriate pride, or low self-esteem.

Can we learn to accept and depend upon God's grace the way Paul did?

> I was given a thorn in my flesh, a messenger of Satan, to torment me. Three times I pleaded with the Lord to take it away from me. But he said to me, "My grace is sufficient for you, for my power is made perfect in weakness." Therefore I will boast all the more gladly about my weaknesses, so that Christ's power may rest on me. That is why, for Christ's sake, I delight in weaknesses, in insults, in hardships, in persecutions, in difficulties. For when I am weak, then I am strong. (2 Corinthians 12:7–10)

What Is the Meaning of Grace?

According to Dictionary.com, *grace* is "a manifestation of favor, especially by a superior." In the Greek, the word *charis* (pronounced like *charisma*) means "to bestow pleasures on; delight or favorable regard."

Many people confuse grace with mercy. Mercy is when God does not give a person the punishment he or she deserves. Grace is when God gives a person a blessing he or she does not deserve. In her book *Embrace Grace*, Liz Curtis Higgs said, "Forgiveness would be gift enough, but God also purifies us—gives us a spiritual bath, scrubs our souls clean—and helps us begin anew. Now that's grace."[17] Liz also gave this explanation, "To redeem a gift certificate, you hand over a piece of paper—purchased by someone else and inscribed with your name—in exchange for something of value yet at no cost to you. You've done nothing to deserve this free gift. You simply hold out your hands and say, 'Thank you.' That's grace in a nutshell. A gift. A gift. With a tag that reads 'For you.'"[18]

Only So Much Room in My Closet

God's grace is there for the taking. We have the choice. Are there old things we need to clean out to accept the new?

I enjoy going to boutiques to find beautiful limited-edition clothing. My rule: If I want to add a new piece to my closet, I have to get rid of something I don't need anymore. For our purpose here, let's say we are shopping at The Grace

---

17. Liz Curtis Higgs, *Embrace Grace* (Colorado Springs: WaterBrook Press, 2006), 78.
18. Curtis Higgs, *Embrace Grace*, 91.

Boutique. We've received a gift card from a very special friend, a thousand dollars to shop at The Grace Boutique! The clothes in our closet have been looking rather used, ragged, and out-of-date. The colors aren't as bright as they once were. There's a lot of black and gray, dull colors that sure could use a lift. We have been given the chance to get rid of the old and bring in the new.

We walk into the boutique and see bright colors, beautiful floral designs, and a crisp newness about every article of clothing. We realize with the free gift card we can replace almost all of the worn-down selections hanging in our closet.

God has purchased us a free gift card to choose all the healing virtues he offers. One of the first notes I penned in my Bible was an acrostic: GRACE (God's Riches At Christ's Expense). The riches God offers come through the expense of Christ's death on the cross. "For God so loved the world that he gave his one and only Son, that whoever believes in him shall not perish but have eternal life" (John 3:16).

Because of Jesus Christ's free gift, we can clean out the anger, selfishness, malice, hate, guilt, and shame from our closet and be clothed differently. Paul put it this way: "Therefore, as God's chosen people, holy and dearly loved, clothe yourselves with compassion, kindness, humility, gentleness and patience. Bear with each other and forgive one another if any of you has a grievance against someone. Forgive as the Lord forgave you. And over all these virtues put on love, which binds them all together in perfect unity" (Colossians 3:12–14).

I wrote the following piece as part of a "Clothed in Christ" workshop presentation:

"Clothing of Christ"

Our Savior, Jesus Christ,
began his life wrapped in a cloth.
He was clothed with compassion in His eyes,
had patience with crowds and criticism,
and loved from His heart.
He wrapped children in His arms and was
clothed as a servant in a towel of humility.
Shod with sandals on His feet,
He shared forgiveness and spoke with
kindness and gentleness.
In death He was clothed in a seamless garment,
purple robe and a crown of thorns.
Jesus was laid to rest wrapped in fine linen and
arose in clothes whiter than snow.
Jesus, thank You for showing us what clothes to wear.

Choosing to wear God's grace-designed clothing will be the very best decision you will ever make in your life. Accept his free gifts. You will feel different, you will look different in the mirror, and others will wonder who did your makeover! With a confident smile, you can reply, "Well, there is this amazing designer who showed me how to change my wardrobe. Let me introduce you to him."

Ripples

Meditate on the one in whom our hope is anchored:

- Emmanuel, God with us (Matthew 1:23)

- Righteous One (Acts 3:14)
- Wonderful Counselor, Mighty God, Everlasting Father, Prince of Peace (Isaiah 9:6)
- The Light of the World (John 8:12; 9:5)
- Father of Compassion and God of all Comfort (2 Corinthians 1:3)
- Full of Mercy (James 3:17)
- Gentle and Humble in Heart (Matthew 11:29)
- My Strength and my Shield (Psalm 28:7)
- My Shepherd, my Guide, and my Hope (John 10:11)
- Jesus, the Radiance of God's Glory (Hebrews 1:3)
- Jesus, what a beautiful name
- Gaze on the beauty of the Lord (Psalm 27:4)
- My Rock, my Fortress, my Deliverer (Psalm 18:2)
- Savior, Redeemer, Lamb of God (John 1:29)
- God's one and only Son sent into the world that we might live through Him (John 3:16)
- The way, the truth, the life (John 14:6)
- The name that is above every name, that at the name of Jesus every knee should bow (Philippians 2:9–10)
- Jesus, the same yesterday, today, and forever (Hebrews 13:8)

I particularly appreciate all the Scripture that is packed into this song of hope.

Endless Hope

Endless hope the gift of grace
When He stepped in and took our place
While we chose to be God's enemy
His love chose to die for me

He washes clean removes my sin
And now His Spirit lives within
Not saved by anything we've done
But the sacrifice of His own Son
Making us heirs of eternal life
Jesus is our Endless Hope

He's the Rock on which I stand
My Strong Tower sheltering me
The Bread of Life, the Living Water
Endless Hope that sets me free

He's my Shepherd guiding me
My Creator, Savior, my Friend
Jehovah Jireh, El Shaddai
Beginning and the End

If God is for us who can be against us?
Endless Hope, the gift of grace
When He stepped in and took our place
While we chose to be God's enemy
His love chose to die for me
Though the earth be removed and
The mountains be cast
Into the greatest depths of the sea
Oh You oh Lord are my Shield
My ever-present help in time of need
If God is for us no evil can stand

If God is for us
Jesus our Endless Hope
Amen[19]

---

19. "Endless Hope," © 2007 Chet A. Chambers. Used by permission.
Words and Music by Chet Chambers, performed by Debbie Roth on *endless HOPE*.

Splashing in the Puddles: Drenched in His Splendor

Sunshine, warmth, walking along a beach, hearing the waves crash against rocks and seagulls singing—what a birthday gift. In September of 2017, we traveled near Sacramento, California, to visit with our daughter, son-in-law, and grandson. Since we were in the area the week of my birthday, I decided it would be a special treat to see the Pacific Ocean.

In the year prior to that trip, I had done a lot of soul searching. I knew that I'd lost my way for a while in my relationship with God. Oh, most people didn't realize I'd been struggling with inner turmoil about past bad decisions. But I knew too well. I finally repented and asked those I'd wronged to forgive me. I was also working through forgiving myself and healing. Finding peace with God, others, and myself was a big part of this time in my life.

Though I generally have summers off, this particular season had been packed. We'd travelled to see family and attend Carol Kent's Speak Up Conference. At the conference, God clearly spoke to my heart about writing a book, the book I said I would never write. Not that I hadn't thought about it, dreamed about it, and heard people say I should, but that summer I felt more convicted than ever about it.

But a painful confrontation happened after the conference that left me confused, hurt beyond what I thought my heart could take, and unsure of not only who I was in Christ but who I was at all. The memories of my upbringing, both good and bad, had been completely contradicted, battered, and shattered. How could I even think about writing a book that drew on these incidents when my memories of them had just been drowned in a wave of hateful accusations? As I drove away from where this had happened, I heard a song on the radio about broken memories. God immediately wrapped his arms around me and began healing me.

He gave me a visual of a large framed picture with snapshots of me since I was a little girl—all of my memories, both the good and bad. He showed me someone taking a mallet to beat and shatter the glass that covered the snapshots. Tears flowed as my memories were taken from me again, but then God showed me, in his grace and mercy, that only the glass was broken. The pictures were still intact. My wonderful memories, and the events that shaped them, were not damaged.

When, on my fifty-ninth birthday, we headed to Ocean Beach in San Francisco, I was able to enjoy the clear sunshine, waves crashing, and seagulls singing. Walking along the beach barefoot and splashing through the waves gently lapping at the shore, I realized that God in his splendor continues to be with us in the drenching storms, the light rain, the puddles left behind, and, yes, the sunshine too.

Refreshing Rest

We cannot protect ourselves from trouble, but we can dance through the puddles of life with a rainbow smile twirling the only umbrella we need—the umbrella of God's love.
—Barbara Johnson

There are just a few scattered sprinkles, parting clouds, and puddles left behind. Clothes are beginning to dry, and you peek out under the umbrella to make sure. The rain has stopped. The numbness in your feet has subsided as you have persevered through the hardest part of the storm. You are thankful the drenching rain has ceased, the sun is peeking through the clouds, and all that is left are puddles.

As a child, I would get excited whenever a rainstorm stopped: "It stopped raining! Can I go outside and play?" Outside, the air smelled fresh, and the sunlight glistened off wet surfaces. Back in the days when it seemed safe to play in the suburban streets (you know with marbles, jacks, or jump ropes), we kids always found the puddles after a good rain. We splashed in them with boots and bare feet and bicycles. We would find the low spots in the yard and splash and pounce in the puddles until they turned to mud.

Being outside was the most refreshing and restful place I could find when I was young. Inside, the house was so full of turmoil. My places of rest were sitting on top of the picnic table, playing on the swings, running through the grass in an open field by our house, and pretending in the playhouse my dad built. Add building snowmen in the winter, and you'll have the complete picture.

When I was around ten, we moved to the country, and I found peace and rest lying in the grass. During the day, I'd busy myself finding four-leaf clovers, and after the sun set, I would gaze at stars. I spent time catching lightning bugs, putting them in glass jars, and watching them glow. The move wasn't the only different thing. I'd grown too. We brought my old playhouse and settled it behind a barn. I had to crouch down to get in the door, but I found it comforting to sit and do homework or read there. In the winter, instead of making mere snowmen, I now created snow sculptures, and my brother and I had a blast pelting each other with snowballs.

I remember when my faith was open and invigorating like that. Oh, to return to those days of childlike faith: fearless, nonjudgmental, honest, joyful, and humble. Looking back, I can see my home was dysfunctional, but I still had enough innocence as a child to trust and find happiness in every day. Matthew 18:1–4 shows us how valued children are in Jesus' eyes: "At that time the disciples came to Jesus and asked, 'Who, then, is the greatest in the kingdom of heaven?' He called a little child to him, and placed the child among them. And he said: 'Truly I tell you, unless you change and become like little children, you will never enter the kingdom of heaven. Therefore, whoever takes the lowly position of this child is the greatest in the kingdom of heaven.'"

Even as a child, I knew my rest and refreshment from experiencing nature was only temporary. Now, although I still love the outdoors, I find my greatest rest not in the creation but in the Creator. To find rest and refreshment in the Lord is to return to that childlike faith, trusting in an awesome God and believing that he will provide love, security, humility, and happiness.

I still love the outdoors. Long walks in all seasons, reading a book on the deck, working in the yard and garden, dates with my husband, and spending time with my children and their children are where God refreshes my soul and helps me find rest. In the middle of winter, I love walking to where an open-water creek runs beside a path and listening to the hundreds of ducks talking to each other and splashing in the water.

Some days, it feels as though there is no time for finding that peace we long for. But like we need rest for our physical bodies, we need rest in our hearts, casting out all fear, worry, and stress and making room for peace, joy, and hope.

I love what David says in Psalm 55: "My heart is in anguish within me; the terrors of death have fallen on me. Fear and trembling have beset me; horror has overwhelmed me. I said, 'Oh, that I had the wings of a dove! I would fly away and be at rest. I would flee far away and stay in the desert; I would hurry to my place of shelter, far from the tempest and storm.' . . . Cast your cares on the LORD and he will sustain you; he will never let the righteous be shaken" (vv. 4–8, 22).

We are able to cast our cares, worries, stress, and fear on the Lord. He provides places of shelter, away from our storms, to allow rest.

I'm sure some of you remember a television commercial advertising a bath product in which a woman exclaimed, "Take me away!" There are times I'd love something to whisk me away to rest, even though my schedule isn't nearly as demanding as Jesus' was. Think about it. In the middle of teaching, preaching, healing, leading, and dining, where did *Jesus* find his rest? How was he able to get away from the crowds, spend time with his disciples, pray, rest, and sleep?

- In calling the first disciples, Jesus walked beside the Sea of Galilee (Matthew 4:18).
- When he saw the crowds, he went up on a mountainside and sat down to teach his disciples (5:1–2).
- Before Jesus calmed a storm, he slept in the boat (8:23–25).
- Jesus sat by the lake, but when the crowds gathered, he moved to a boat (13:1–2).
- When he was told that John the Baptist had been killed, Jesus withdrew by boat privately to a solitary place (14:13).
- Before Jesus walked on water, he spent time on a mountainside, talking with his Father (v. 23).

If the Son of God felt it was necessary at times to withdraw and rest, I think it's safe to say you and I should be doing the same.

Finding Our Place of Refreshing Rest through Jesus Christ
Jesus Christ invites us to focus on him, surrendering our weariness and burdens: "Come to me, all you who are weary and burdened, and I will give you rest. Take my yoke upon you and learn from me, for I am gentle and humble in heart, and you will find rest for your souls. For my yoke is easy and my burden is light" (Matthew 11:28–30).

In our times of pain, despair, grief, fear, busyness, and idleness, our minds need to focus on God. How? We can find refreshment and rest by praying, reading his Word, being still, and listening. In the stillness, with our focus on God, our bodies can sleep better, and we can find refreshment in positive thoughts and intimacy with the Lord. Consider:

- "When you pray, go into your room, close the door and pray to your Father, who is unseen" (Matthew 6:6).
- "The name of the LORD is a strong tower, the righteous run to it and are safe" (Proverbs 18:10).
- "Be still, and know that I am God" (Psalm 46:10).
- "He leads me beside quiet waters, he refreshes my soul" (Psalm 23:2–3).
- "Truly my soul finds rest in God; my salvation comes from him. Truly he is my rock and my salvation; he is my fortress, I will never be shaken" (Psalm 62:1–2).
- "Cast all your anxiety on him because he cares for you" (1 Peter 5:7).

Finding Refreshing Rest through Friends

If you're like me, it helps to have more than God's presence. It's good to have a flesh-and-blood friend at your side too. Refreshment can also be provided by others:

- "Like cold water to a weary soul is good news from a distant land" (Proverbs 25:25).
- "Then, by the will of God, I will be able to come to you with a joyful heart, and we will be an encouragement to each other" (Romans 15:32 NLT).
- "Your love has given me great joy and encouragement, because you, brother, have refreshed the hearts of the Lord's people" (Philemon 1:7).
- "May the Lord show mercy to the household of Onesiphorus because he often refreshed me and was not ashamed of my chains" (2 Timothy 1:16).

To close out this chapter on rest, I would like to share about a very special woman. I met Toni when she was the worship leader for our congregation. She was passionate for God and his music, and she had the most beautiful, radiant smile. Wife to Tim and mother to three wonderful boys, she passed away on the evening of October 14, 2015, after an eight-year battle with metastatic breast cancer. What follows is Toni's last CaringBridge journal entry. Refreshment came from her family and friends, and there is no doubt rest came about because she allowed God's comforting arms to wrap around her.

Hello Friends and Family,

We are about to close the 26th day of hospice care. Please know that all your prayers, visits, fabulous food, excursions for the boys, and so many other things are holding us up and holding us together during this time. It was not an easy decision to make, but I know in my heart that it was the right one for me. I'm focused on *quality of life* now. And I can't tell you the difference it feels not to be running to so many appointments but to be spending time with my boys, my hubby, and so many of you who have come to offer a hand with the housework, hugs, prayers, or songs!

We've enjoyed the company of so much of our immediate family, including my parents, both of my brothers, my Godmother and some cousins, and my bestie from all the way back to...WOW! 8th grade... as 'live-ins,' as well as each of Tim's siblings, even Natalie and her husband and 3 beautiful girls from L.A. We've enjoyed watching Facebook light up with lots of encouraging words from family and friends across the world! And I'm going on record to say that I have the BEST High School Graduating Class on the Planet! Go Homer Central High School, Class of 1991 Trojans!

I'm holding together relatively well. The hospice care team assigned to us is great keeping me as comfortable as possible. Medications are constantly needing to be looked at to keep my anxiety down and my breathing more fluid. I'm thankful for my special team of spiritual friends and guides who help me prepare for the Glory that awaits me. The balance there is difficult–wanting so much to be with Jesus and digging in my heels and wanting to stay here with my boys like I had planned all those years. But the word to notice there is I, not He. It is God's Will, not mine, that is the best ending to this and all stories. I will ask for your prayers to help me remember to continually ask for and accept His Will for me. It cannot be a bad ending if He is in charge. It has to be beautiful.[20]

Ripples

Where have the places of rest been in your life?

As a child:

As a teen:

As an adult:

Find the refreshing rest in these Scriptures:
- Acts 3:19
- Proverbs 3
- John 14
- Philippians 4:4–9

As a teenager, my husband wrote the following song the day after a family in his home church was killed in an auto accident. It's been carrying its message of resting in the Lord to audiences ever since.

---

20. Toni Diem, "It Has to Be Beautiful," August 10, 2015, https://www.caringbridge.org/visit/tonidiem/journal. Used by permission.

Gentle Communion

Gentle communion
Just a walk with my Savior
I talked to sweet Jesus
And I thanked Him for the words
He told me He loved me
Then He sat down beside me
Said here is My shoulder
Now go ahead and cry
And I cried

Lord, I'm so tired
I been runnin' for a long time
Wind don't blow
And the rain don't shine
But You've heard those words before
Jesus, I thank You for Your hand
And Your shoulder
Your hand moved my boulder
And Your shoulder dried my eyes.

Gentle communion
How it grows with the seasons
Bringing more peace
Than any tongue could tell
All of my failures
Sideswipes and sorrows
Fears of tomorrows
Regrets of yesterday
Drift away when I say

Lord I'm so tired
I been runnin' for a long time
Wind don't blow
And the rain don't shine
But You've heard those words before
Jesus, I thank You for Your hand
And Your shoulder
Your hand moved my boulder
And Your shoulder dried my eyes[21]

21. "Gentle Communion," © 1974 Music GGGGus. Used by permission. Words and Music by Dewey Roth, performed by Debbie and Dewey Roth on *endless HOPE*.

Worship

The deepest level of worship is praising God in spite of pain, trusting Him during a trial, surrendering while suffering, and loving Him when He seems distant.
—Rick Warren

Fly like a bird!

Whenever I was asked the question, "If you could be any animal, what would you be?" my answer was always, "A bird." I always wished I could soar above everything here on earth, above all the pain and heartache, and fly where peace resides.

The morning of my fiftieth birthday, I found a card in my makeup bag. The envelope held a picture of a skydiver and—to my surprise—a gift certificate for skydiving.

My husband wanted to celebrate my fiftieth birthday, fifty pounds lost, and ten years cancer-free. He'd contacted friends and family to see if they wanted to contribute to the gift, and he planned to host an open house honoring those three events. (The highlight of the evening would be watching the video from my skydiving adventure.)

I was going to fly like a bird! We reached the skydiving location, watched a video on the dangers, signed a liability waiver, and got suited up to jump out of "a perfectly good airplane." (Later, I was told there is no such thing as a perfectly good airplane.) I never felt anxious, only excited about floating in the sky like a bird. I was thankful for the confident tandem instructor, and the strong rigging that attached us together.

There was rain in the area that day, so they chose a time between clouds when we could jump at the highest altitude possible. We rolled out of the airplane, and during the freefall, I realized it was sprinkling and raindrops were hitting the goggles. (After landing, I used my fingers as wipers over the goggles. Do we have trouble seeing God clearly because of the rain/pain in our lives? There is no doubt God has been the wipers on my goggles, allowing me to see him through the pain.) When the parachute opened, we floated and soared just like a bird. It was the most incredible feeling ever.

My first thoughts were "God, you are amazing!" and "Dad, can you see me?" It all happened so fast, but I was able to experience a tiny piece of the grandeur that God designed. Two years later, I was struck by that awe again when I jumped from a higher altitude just before sunset. Seeing more of God's creation ignited worship. N. T. Wright says, "The closer you get to the truth, the clearer becomes the beauty, and the more you will find worship welling up within you."[22]

---

22. N. T. Wright, *For All God's Worth: True Worship and the Calling of the Church* (Grand Rapids: Wm. B. Eerdmans Publishing, 2014), 12.

Worship comes easily in certain situations: being over-whelmed with the beauty of nature, being healed from a sickness, or seeing a loved one accept Christ. Worship might not be so easy when your loved one has been diagnosed with a disease such as cancer. You're looking for reasons to hope, and the doctors say there are none.

It's at those times when you don't *feel* like worshiping but take the time to acknowledge God's greatness anyway that worship ends up helping you get through your struggles. When we tell God we trust him, we remind ourselves that he is trustworthy. When we express our faith in God, we reinforce to ourselves that he is faithful.

There is more than one way to worship. And if you're thinking, "Singing isn't really my thing. I can't worship God all that well," it is time to expand your horizons and get out of that narrow definition of what worship is. Celebrating the "worthship" of God—connecting with your heavenly Father personally and with a clean conscience—can include a lot more than singing. In fact, even though I love music and have been deeply affected by particular songs, singing may very well be the last thing on the agenda.

May this chapter help you appreciate activities that you may not have considered to be "worship." Surrender your heart and mind to the one who created you, be filled with wonder and adoration, and then turn your inner worship and awe into exuberant outward praise.

Solitude and Silence

In chapter 7, we discussed how Jesus found his solitude by spending time away from the crowds and his disciples, usually on a mountainside or near water. He would retreat to a place where he could be alone, without distractions, praying fervently and listening to how his Father responded.

In today's world, we often wake up and immediately start thinking about our schedule for the day. Our to-do list captures our attention, and in our minds, we have completed our day before beginning. And as much as we appreciate cell phones and the availability of instant connection, we find ourselves tied to devices, constantly checking them for messages. If we're involved in social media, the interactions with others (both positive and negative) soak up time, leaving us with even fewer hours in the day and filling our minds and hearts with one situation after another and a busload of possible responses.

Retreating to a quiet place allows us to clear our hearts and minds of the negativity that can pull us away from truly worshiping God. Psalm 46:10 says, "Be still, and know that I am God." Notice that it doesn't say, "Get busy, and know that I am God."

In his song "Take My Life," Scott Underwood wrote about surrendering to God: "Take my heart and form it. Take my mind; transform it. Take my will; conform it to Yours."[23] It sounds a lot like David: "Teach me your way, Lord, that I may rely on your faithfulness; give me an undivided heart, that I may fear your name" (Psalm 86:11).

Maybe it's so obvious that you've never thought about it, but we tend to find what we look for. We tend to see what

---

23. "Take My Life (Holiness),"©1995 Vineyard Music. Used by permission. Words and Music by Scott Underwood.

we are thinking about it. (I know that when I was expecting each of our four children, it seemed like every other woman at the mall was also pregnant.) Imagine the positive effect on our spirits when we make an effort to focus on God: "Look to the LORD and his strength; seek his face always" (Psalm 105:4).

In your time of silence, imagine Jesus sitting across from you. Look into his eyes and allow his love to saturate your heart and mind. When we think we are alone, he says, "I am with you." When the truth is burning to be told, he says, "I already know, but I still want to listen." When we feel unlovable, Jesus says, "I love you." When going on seems impossible, he looks into our eyes, takes our hands, and says, "Press on. I am here to carry your burden. Follow me."

To be in God's presence, assured of his love and forgiveness, is nothing short of glorious. "True worship can't hide anything. To worship in spirit and in truth means nothing is hidden."[24]

Prayer

What a gift it is to be able to travel on the two-way street we call prayer. According to singer-songwriter Rich Mullins, "Prayer is a grace through which we pour ourselves out before God and through which He calls us into His presence."[25]

If you've been around church folks long enough, you may be familiar with an outline for our prayers that uses the acronym ACTS, which stands for Adoration, Confession,

---

24. Bill Johnson, "What is Worship?," https://app.worshipu.com/library/what-is-worship.
25. Rich Mullins, http://www.azquotes.com/quote/734043.

Thanksgiving, and Supplication. For our purposes here, I like what James L. Nicodem said in his book *Prayer Coach*:

> Although ACTS has been a helpful tool for me to use over the years, I've often felt that this acronym could be improved upon. For starters, who even knows what *supplication* means anymore? Let's replace that with a better word. Next, there are times when I just can't begin my praying with *adoration* because I'm feeling dirtied by my sin and distant from God. But if I deal with this problem by launching my prayer with *confession*, this would change the acronym to CATS. As a dog lover, I just can't go there. Finally, ACTS, as a word, has nothing to do with prayer. Let me suggest a new acronym that does: CHAT. When it's time to talk (i.e., chat) with God, I am reminded to balance my prayer with four emphases (stated as verbs here to give them a sense of action). Confess. Honor (for *adoration*). Ask (beats *supplication* any day). Thank.[26]

Confess

Surrender yourself and become humble before God. Give to him your anger, pride, selfishness, disrespect, anxiety, worldly passions, greed, and hate.

When we empty ourselves, God has room to breathe into us his forgiveness, humility, compassion, gentleness, peace, patience, self-control, thankfulness, and love.

But don't take my word for it. Consider the examples and encouragements found in the Scriptures:

---

26. James L. Nicodem, *Prayer Coach* (Wheaton, IL: Crossway Books, 2008), 100.

- "Have mercy on me, O God, according to your unfailing love; according to your great compassion blot out my transgressions. Wash away all my iniquity and cleanse me from my sin. For I know my transgressions, and my sin is always before me" (Psalm 51:1–3).
- "Then I acknowledged my sin to you and did not cover up my iniquity. I said, 'I will confess my transgressions to the Lord'—and you forgave the guilt of my sin. Therefore let all the faithful pray to you while you may be found; surely the rising of the mighty waters will not reach them. You are my hiding place; you will protect me from trouble and surround me with songs of deliverance" (Psalm 32:5–7).
- "If we confess our sins, he is faithful and just and will forgive us our sins and purify us from all unrighteousness" (1 John 1:9).

Honor

Why would we pray to God at all if we didn't know him as someone far mightier, more loving, and infinitely wiser than we are? Verbally honoring God for who he is isn't for God's benefit. He doesn't have a poor self-image. He doesn't need our words to lift him out of depression. No, honoring God with our lips helps us! It reminds us what kind of person we are worshiping.

Let these scriptural examples prime the pump for your prayers:

- "Come, let us bow down in worship, let us kneel before the LORD our Maker; for he is our God and we

are the people of his pasture, the flock under his care"
(Psalm 95:6–7).

- "Ascribe to the LORD, you heavenly beings, ascribe
  to the LORD glory and strength. Ascribe to the LORD
  the glory due his name; worship the LORD in the
  splendor of his holiness. The voice of the LORD is
  over the waters; the God of glory thunders, the LORD
  thunders over the mighty waters. The voice of the
  LORD is powerful; the voice of the LORD is majestic"
  (Psalm 29:1–4).

- "Great is the LORD and most worthy of praise; his
  greatness no one can fathom. One generation com-
  mends your works to another; they tell of your
  mighty acts. They speak of the glorious splendor of
  your majesty, and I will meditate on your wonderful works. They tell of the power of your awesome
  works, and I will proclaim your great deeds. They
  celebrate your abundant goodness and joyfully sing
  of your righteousness" (Psalm 145:3–7).

Ask

This is the part of prayer most people immediately think of,
right? The average person on the street, when confronted
with the concept of prayer, will equate it with asking God
for things. The great truth is that God says that's perfectly
fine. When balanced with the other aspects of prayer, asking
is a healthy part of our relationship with our loving heavenly
Father:

- "If my people, who are called by my name, will humble themselves and pray and seek my face and turn

from their wicked ways, then I will hear from heaven, and I will forgive their sin and will heal their land" (2 Chronicles 7:14).

- "Ask and it will be given to you; seek and you will find; knock and the door will be opened to you" (Matthew 7:7).

- "Which of you, if your son asks for bread, will give him a stone? Or if he asks for a fish, will give him a snake? If you, then, though you are evil, know how to give good gifts to your children, how much more will your Father in heaven give good gifts to those who ask him!" (Matthew 7:9–11).

- "Do not be anxious about anything, but in every situation, by prayer and petition, with thanksgiving, present your requests to God. And the peace of God, which transcends all understanding, will guard your hearts and your minds in Christ Jesus" (Philippians 4:6–7).

Thank

We recently celebrated the fourth birthday of our grandson Thomas. As he excitedly opened his presents, it was clear that he had been coached by Mommy and Daddy how to properly respond to being given a gift: "What do you say, Thomas?"

"Thank you."

It shouldn't be any different for us. Remembering to thank the Lord for his goodness towards us reinforces our relationship with him and reminds us that "every good and perfect gift is from above" (James 1:17):

- "I will give thanks to you, LORD, with all my heart; I will tell of all your wonderful deeds" (Psalm 9:1).
- Jesus' example: "Taking the five loaves and the two fish and looking up to heaven, he gave thanks and broke them. Then he gave them to the disciples to distribute to the people" (Luke 9:16).
- "Give thanks in all circumstances; for this is God's will for you in Christ Jesus" (1 Thessalonians 5:18).

Serving Others

We'll get into this more in section 4, but for now, briefly consider how we worship God when we stop focusing on ourselves and do good things for others. At the very least, we're following the example of Jesus. At the very most, we're serving Christ himself:

> Then the King will say to those on his right, "Come, you who are blessed by my Father; take your inheritance, the kingdom prepared for you since the creation of the world. For I was hungry and you gave me something to eat, I was thirsty and you gave me something to drink, I was a stranger and you invited me in, I needed clothes and you clothed me, I was sick and you looked after me, I was in prison and you came to visit me."
>
> Then the righteous will answer him, "Lord, when did we see you hungry and feed you, or thirsty and give you something to drink? When did we see you a stranger and invite you in, or needing clothes and clothe you? When did we see you sick or in prison and go to visit you?"
>
> The King will reply, "Truly I tell you, whatever you did for one of the least of these brothers and sisters of mine, you did for me." (Matthew 25:34–40)

Giving

When a church deacon or usher passes an offering plate or basket or bucket, they're not just asking for money to keep the lights on and pay the pastor's salary. This is an opportunity to worship. When we let go of our "hard earned cash," we are expressing our trust in God and reinforcing our relationship with him. We are saying, "I know you love me and are dedicated to causing all things to work out for good." We are saying we believe God's Word:

- "I was young and now I am old, yet I have never seen the righteous forsaken or their children begging bread" (Psalm 37:25).
- "On the first day of every week, each one of you should set aside a sum of money in keeping with your income" (1 Corinthians 16:2).
- "I have received from Epaphroditus the gifts you sent. They are a fragrant offering, an acceptable sacrifice, pleasing to God. And my God will meet all your needs according to the riches of his glory in Christ Jesus" (Philippians 4:18–19).

When we're in the middle of the kinds of pain and struggles we've been talking about, worshiping God may not be the first thing we think about doing, but we have to have a relationship with him in order to receive his grace and experience his promises. These are all acts of faith that will be rewarded by a heavenly Father who loves to give good things to his children.

Ripples

The following is an A–Z list of some of the attributes, names, and titles of God. Choose a few each time you pray, taking time to meditate on how those aspects of God have affected your life. Repeat them back to God, and honor and praise him with your whole heart:

Almighty

Bread of Life

Comforter

Dwelling place

Everlasting

Fountain of life

Gracious

Hope

Intercessor

Just

Kind

Light of the World

Mighty God

Name above all names

One and only

Prince of Peace

Quieter (the one who quiets my soul)

Resting place

Savior

Thirst quencher

Unchanging

Victor

Wisdom

X-alted

Yahweh

Zion's King

This song was written by a friend and a studio engineer for my third CD. It captures the intent of us pouring ourselves out to God, being transparent before our Creator.

We Look to You

Still waters run deep
Like the promises You keep

These waters wash the pain
Your love pours like rain
When things get in the way
And I'm living day to day
I remember what You say
And my aching goes away

And we look to You for comfort
We look to You for grace
We look to You for healing
We look to see Your face
And then You find our open hearts, Lord
Forgiving everything
Please open up our hearts, Lord
So we can give this back today

Deep waters run still
Come and drink your fill
They'll take away the pain
Your love pours like rain
Hurt will sometimes blind me
And I know just what to do
I look to what is true
To the healing words from You

Sometimes I forget just who I am
But I'm reminded every day
It's a part of Your plan
Still the waters run deep
Like the promises You keep
In these waters pain won't breathe
As your love pours like rain
And Your love heals all pain

. . . And then we find Your open arms, Lord
Forgiving everything
Please open up our hearts, Lord
So we can give this back today[27]

---

27. "We Look to You," © 2009 John Fox and Nathan Heironimus. Used by permission. Words and Music by John Fox and Nathan Heironimus, performed by Debbie Roth on *drenched in HOPE.*

9

Basking in God's Provisions: Drenched in Hope

Worrying is carrying tomorrow's load with today's strength—carrying two days at once. It is moving into tomorrow ahead of time. Worrying doesn't empty tomorrow of its sorrow, it empties today of its strength.

—Corrie ten Boom

On a Monday, I received a card in the mail from the doctor's office stating all looked good on the mammogram. "We will see you next year!" Two days later, I received another card saying the same thing. I thought it was rather strange that I received two cards with the information I was hoping for, not just one.

I work at a school on a stretch calendar, which means there are several weeks throughout the school year that we have off. This was one of those weeks. I had decided to take a substitute paraprofessional position at another school that Friday. Rushing, I grabbed the car keys and my lunch and was just about to head downstairs to leave when the phone rang. I almost didn't answer, but I decided it might be a call from the substitute office, giving me more information or saying they didn't need me after all. As it turned out, it was the doctor's office, and they said I needed to report to the St. Paul Medical Building for a magnified mammogram. What? Very confused, I told the caller about the two cards in the mail that week saying all was clear and they would see me in a year. The doctor's secretary said a third radiologist looked over the mammograms (not only from that year but a couple years prior also) and realized there was a significant difference, showing that my left breast was probably full of cancer. I called the school immediately to let them know I wouldn't be coming in.

I walked out to the mailbox for some reason, and a neighbor was there at the same time. I looked at him and said, "I just found out I probably have cancer." Shock, confusion, and a mental numbness all set in.

I don't remember much more about that day or the days immediately after it, but on Monday, with help from a friend from church, I made my way in for the test. Upon completion, they handed me a file with the pictures from the mammogram and told me to show them to the doctor. I had a friend who worked in radiology, and she came over to look at the pictures. I wanted to know what she saw. She pointed out many locations of what was probably cancer.

After meeting with the doctor, a biopsy was scheduled for further testing. During the needle-localized procedure, they had a hard time figuring out which section to take the sample from because there were so many. Somehow, the medical staff and I were able to laugh about that.

A few days later, one of the teachers at my school came and got me while I was on a class outing in the community. She told me the surgeon's office had called. Now, the surgeon had told me if the nurse called with the results then we would be good to schedule a checkup months later, but if *he* called, we needed to talk right away. When I asked if it was the nurse or the surgeon, I could tell the answer by her face.

For this type of cancer, my options were limited: Take one breast to get rid of the cancer that was present, or take both, hoping to prevent the cancer from showing up again later. I was also told that had the third radiologist not seen what he saw, I would definitely have been fighting for my life within a couple months. On December 4, 1998, they took both breasts, and I began a long road of recovery.

Some will read that story and think, "How tragic!" Not me. Scattered throughout my journey with breast cancer are instances of God clearly providing for my well-being:

- The third radiologist
- The friend who worked in radiology and prepared my heart for what I was about to hear
- The smiles during the biopsy procedure
- A surgeon whose name was Dr. Hope
- Compassionate coworkers
- A good friend who flew into town through the night to be there for the surgery (Her mom passed away from breast cancer a year earlier.)
- Beautiful greetings from friends and family through cards and books
- Prayers, so many prayers
- A wonderful daughter who was there for her siblings while their daddy was taking care of me (Months before any of this happened, she turned down a full-ride scholarship to a college in Cincinnati and decided to attend a school only twenty minutes away.)

- A husband who could be with me during the days of my recovery (He resigned from vocational ministry months earlier, and we weren't all that thrilled the job he landed was third shift, but that's how God provided a way for him to be home during the day to nurse me through. For your information, I don't believe in coincidences.)

Though survivor's guilt sets in now and then when I see someone struggling with cancer a whole lot harder than I did, I am thankful to be able to share my story and truly feel compassion for others in their storms.

Whether in the deep trials of life or the everyday moments, God provides what we need. It may not always seem like it though, and sometimes we feel powerless. It's then we need to step inside the provisions and abilities of Jesus. In the words of Corrie ten Boom, "When we are powerless to do a thing, it is a great joy that we can come and step inside the ability of Jesus."[28]

I'm so grateful for eyes to see how God provides what we need. What are some of those provisions we can only find through him?

The Armor of God

In Ephesians 6:10–17, Paul spelled out a way to "be strong in the Lord and in his mighty power" (v. 10). We are able to

---

28. Corrie ten Boom, *Jesus is Victor* (Grand Rapids, MI: Fleming H. Revell Co., 1985), 89.

stand firm regardless what comes our way by putting on the armor of God:

- The belt of truth
- The breastplate of righteousness
- "Feet fitted with the readiness that comes from the gospel of peace" (v. 15)
- The shield of faith
- The helmet of salvation
- The sword of the Spirit, the word of God

Fruit of the Spirit

In Galatians 5:22–23, we find the result of being led by the Holy Spirit:

- Love
- Joy
- Peace
- Patience
- Kindness
- Goodness
- Faithfulness
- Gentleness
- Self-control

Rescue and Protection

"Because he loves me," says the LORD, "I will rescue him;
I will protect him, for he acknowledges my name.
He will call upon me, and I will answer him;
I will be with him in trouble,
I will deliver him and honor him.

With long life will I satisfy him
And show him my salvation."
(Psalm 91:14–16)

Strength

Do you not know? Have you not heard?
The LORD is the everlasting God,
The Creator of the ends of the earth.
He will not grow tired or weary,
And his understanding no one can fathom.
He gives strength to the weary
And increases the power of the weak.
Even youths grow tired and weary,
And young men stumble and fall;
But those who hope in the LORD will renew their
strength.
They will soar on wings like eagles;
They will run and not grow weary,
They will walk and not be faint.
(Isaiah 40:28–31)

In Christ We Have . . .

A love that can never be fathomed,
A life that can never die,
A righteousness that can never be tarnished,
A peace that can never be understood,
A rest that can never be disturbed,
A joy that can never be diminished,
A hope that can never be disappointed,
A glory that can never be clouded,
A light that can never be darkened,

A purity that can never be defiled,
A beauty that can never be marred,
A wisdom that can never be baffled,
Resources that can never be exhausted.
Jesus is our all in all![29]

Other God-Given Provisions

God will never force himself or his gifts upon you. He makes these promised provisions available, but it takes our choice and effort to enjoy them in everyday life:

- The Bible—despite centuries of abuse and people trying to erase it from existence, God's Word remains!
- Christian publications—while we should never confuse the words of people like Max Lucado or Anne Graham Lotz (or Debbie Roth) with Scripture, there are words of wisdom between the covers of many books.
- Christian friends—"A friend loves at all times, and a brother is born for a time of adversity" (Proverbs 17:17).
- Christian community—remember that "church" is not a place you go; it's a group of people to whom you belong. There are no examples in Scripture of a "Lone Ranger" Christian; we were never meant to spend our lives alone.
- Music that honors God—"Music acts like a magic key, to which the most tightly closed heart opens."[30]

---

29. Unknown, "In Christ We Have", https://bible.org/illustration/christ-we-have.
30. Maria von Trapp, http://www.azquotes.com/quote/353964.

Above all, know this. Know that God is in our storms, under our umbrella, brushing the tears away so we can see and keeping our feet moving forward. When numbness sets in, he walks in our shoes with us. God is in the parting clouds, the sunshine, and even the puddles. Return to your childlike faith and splash in the puddles once again.

Ripples
How has God provided ways for you to get through difficult times in your life?

Has there been a life circumstance that, at the time, seemed unfortunate but ended up being a positive thing?
Spend some time in thanksgiving right now.

I was blessed to be able to contribute to the writing of the title song for my third CD project, from which this book also gets its title.

Drenched in Hope

(water) Sometimes raging seas at times a parched dry land
(water) Can be a flood or showers helping things to grow
(water) Life sustaining yet sometimes takes away
Your outpouring overflowing
overwhelming waves of love

Like the ocean in a teacup
Like a river that can't be tamed

Sometimes floating
Sometimes drowning in Your flood
Where there's dirt there can be cleansing
Where there's thirst there is quenching
Grace pours out
Mercy rains down
Your love flows, and I am drenched in hope
(pouring) Your blood Your life poured out for me
(raining) Blessings undeserved raining down on me
(flowing) Streams of living water flow from You
through me
Your drenching quenching rippling roaring
Sustaining waves of love[31]

---

31. "Drenched in Hope," © 2009 Chet A. Chambers and Debbie Roth. Used by permission. Words and Music Chet Chambers and Debbie Roth, performed by Debbie Roth on *drenched in HOPE*.

Sharing under the Rainbow: Drenched in Sonshine

S itting in his small office in Muncie, Indiana, my Christian counselor, Charley, looked me in the eye and said, "You should write a book."

My mom had passed; I had become a five-year cancer survivor; and I was feeling totally waterlogged from the storms of my forty-five years of life. I went to Charley in search of words of wisdom, and that was apparently the best he could do.

"Charley, I don't write books and wouldn't even know where to start," I replied.

"Ah, but you sing."

Thankfully, he didn't push more about the writing, and those four short words—"Ah, but you sing"—began my journey of ministering to others with music. I wanted to comfort others with the comfort I had received from God, and music had certainly been a significant part of that.

A great friend had a recording studio in his house. We used prerecorded accompaniment tracks to put together some songs on a CD to be used as a tool in my hands to comfort others with God's encouragement. The songs were those that had spoken strongly to me of God's love, compassion, forgiveness, and hope.

When God equips you for ministry, you can be sure he will give you opportunities to use that equipment. I immediately began encountering people who needed a loving touch from God. Within a month's time, the CDs ran out. (When using prerecorded tracks, you can only make so many copies legally.) My friend encouraged me to find another set of songs to record; then we repeated the process. Once again, the CDs ran through my hands like a silk scarf, speaking hope to others' pain.

In the fall of 2004, I met with Charley again. He said I needed something a bit more professional to get God's message, the saving grace of Jesus and the hope we have in him, out to more people. The first professional studio I contacted didn't really understand my vision for creating these musical tools of hope. (Because the plan wasn't to make money, they just didn't get it.) I turned my attention to another studio in Fort Wayne, Indiana. When I checked their website, I found a producer who was a worship leader at his church. We made contact, and I learned that we had friends in common. Also, the church he attended was the same church my husband served in his first youth ministry.

Coincidence? I like to call it "God-incidence."

So a teenage dream came true. I was recording in a professional studio! Of course, as a teenager, I never thought I'd be recording music to share God's hope. (And perhaps an even bigger surprise was that what started as a single CD grew into four.)

In the fall of 2005, Rest In Him Ministry began as a non-profit organization. God took me on a journey I could never have imagined. He used my life story and his redemption story to spread his compassion, love, peace, and hope to women, congregations, prisoners, and even people attending the Minnesota State Fair.

After singing and speaking for over ten years, I could still hear Charley saying, "You should write a book." And you're holding in your hands the result of those *five* short words.

1|0

Misery to Ministry

Courageously joyful people . . . have anchored their hearts to the shoreline of God. Will the boat rock? Yes. Will moods come and go? No doubt. But will they be left adrift on the Atlantic of despair? No, for they have found a joy which remains courageous through the storm. And this courageous joy is quick to become a contagious joy.

—Max Lucado

God has brought me through the storms thus far. There is no reason to believe he won't continue to be with me during any others that may come my way. I can look back and see how over the years—yes, even as a child—God was my protector and afforded me joy and the strength to carry on. After I learned that Jesus died for me on the cross and was resurrected to new life, I continued to survive because of his compassion, love, peace, comfort, and hope.

I choose to remember how exciting it felt, as a small child, when I was able to water ski, spend time with Edy next door, play outside, and have family holidays with the neighbors every year. From my teen years, I choose to remember wonderful vacations at Grandma and Grandpa's house, water skiing on the weekends, choir concerts, and great friends. And now, as an adult, God has given me so much to be thankful for: a loving, God-fearing husband, Christian in-laws who took me in as their very own, four beautiful children, their spouses, and amazing grandchildren.

There are still rainstorms. I still get pretty wet from time to time, but I have learned that God is there. He is the Mighty Fortress who can withstand any gale-force winds that come our way. His arms are wrapped around us at all times, making sure we don't get overwhelmed by the drenching waters and carrying us to the rainbow of promise and beyond to eternal *Son*shine. All we need to do is trust his heart, continue to worship him, and acknowledge him as our Lord and Savior. We know he has all the answers.

God's request of us? Share him. Share him through our stories—the bad and the good.

Like It Says in the Bible . . .

At this point, you shouldn't be surprised to know there are scriptural examples of what I'm talking about.

The Woman at the Well

The whole story is in John 4:4–42, and we looked at the highlights already in chapter 2, but here's a quick recap with a new focus:

- A woman is at the well outside of town midday, not in the cool of the morning or evening when the other women would gather there to get the day's water and the latest gossip. Why? Probably because she was the topic of the gossip.
- Jesus starts a conversation with the woman by asking her for a drink of water. This is unusual because she's

a woman *and* a Samaritan. Either of these attributes would keep a normal Jewish man of the first century from having a conversation with her, but of course, Jesus isn't a normal Jewish man.

- The conversation leads to Jesus letting her know that he knows about her shady past and disreputable present and, in spite of that, offering her the living water of the Spirit.
- The woman runs into town and invites the people there to come and check out Jesus for themselves.
- "Many of the Samaritans from that town believed in him because of the woman's testimony" (v. 39).

It's an excellent pattern: Receive love and acceptance from Jesus, then pass it on to others.

The Man Born Blind
Here are the pertinent points from his story found in John 9:1–41:

- Jesus gives sight to a man who was born blind.
- The Pharisees are upset about this because it was done on the Sabbath, when no one was supposed to do any work.
- The Pharisees launch an investigation and, while questioning the formerly blind man, try to get him to recant his former statement that Jesus was a prophet.
- The man replies, "Whether he is a sinner or not, I don't know. One thing I do know. I was blind but now I see!" (v. 25).

- The Pharisees are frustrated in their efforts to discredit Jesus.
- The man worships Jesus.

It's not too much to ask, is it? As Jesus told another man after casting demons out of him and into a herd of pigs, "Return home and tell how much God has done for you" (Luke 8:39). It's not a bunch of theology. It's just telling our stories.

How the Four CDs Line Up

If you've visited my website (www.RestInHimMinistry.com), you may have seen the progression of the four *HOPE* music projects compared to living through a traumatic medical diagnosis. What if we use the storm metaphor from this book?

only HOPE in the storm

A powerful thunderstorm hits you with its full force. A flash flood threatens to sweep you away. You desperately call out to God because you've got nowhere else to turn.

endless HOPE

The initial shock of the storm front has passed over you, but the wind is still strong, and your strength is being tested. You anchor yourself to the strongest thing around: the promises of God.

drenched in HOPE

The worst is over. There are beams of light bursting through the clouds, and you are in awe of both the Creator's power and providential care.

living letters of HOPE

You know just because that storm is over doesn't mean there won't be others. And you know people around you either are or soon will be experiencing their own flash floods and hurricanes. It's time to let them know how you got through and how they can too.

Ripples

How do you relate to the following verses? Do they feel encouraging . . . or convicting?

- "Everyone who calls on the name of the Lord will be saved. How, then, can they call on the one they have not believed in? And how can they believe in the one of whom they have not heard? And how can they hear without someone preaching to them? And how can anyone preach unless they are sent? As it is written: 'How beautiful are the feet of those who bring good news'" (Romans 10:13–15).
- "In your hearts revere Christ as Lord. Always be prepared to give an answer to everyone who asks you to give the reason for the hope that you have" (1 Peter 3:15).
- "You yourselves are our letter, written on our hearts, known and read by everyone. You show that you are a letter from Christ, the result of our ministry, written not with ink but with the Spirit of the living God, not on tablets of stone but on tablets of human hearts" (2 Corinthians 3:2–3).

Living Letters of Hope

She's at the well drawing water, again all alone
Jesus came near
He knew things about her He couldn't have known
She ran into town saying, "This is the One.
He told me everything I'd ever done
Now my life is changed and I tell you that
He is the Son of God!"

She was a letter, a living letter
Not lifeless ink on yellowed pages
But proof of truth for the ages
A letter, a living letter
Just when she reached the end of her rope
She became
A living letter of hope

He said he'd been blind since the day of his birth
He'd been begging for bread
He had no sense of his worth
Jesus walked by and opened his eyes
But the ones who should've seen said, "It's just a lie"
The man said, "All I know is once I was blind,
But now I see."

He was a letter, a living letter
Not lifeless ink on yellowed pages
But proof of truth for the ages
A letter, a living letter
Just when he reached the end of his rope

He became
A living letter of hope
God takes the ones who are broken
And sick and can't cope
He rewrites the story of our lives into
Living letters of hope

We are all letters, we're living letters
Not lifeless ink on yellowed pages
We're proof of truth for the ages
We're letters, we're living letters
Just when we reach the end of our rope
We become
Living letters of hope[32]

---

32. "Living Letters of Hope," © 2011 Music GGGGus and Chet A. Chambers. Used by permission. Words and Music Dewey Roth, Chet Chambers, and Nathan Heironimus, performed by Debbie Roth on *living letters of HOPE*.

Sweet Encouragement

If you give it to God, He transforms your test into a testimony, your mess into a message, and your misery into a ministry.

—Rick Warren

"God, please show me someone who could use your promise of hope on this flight."

Whenever I fly, I always carry onboard a few of my CDs, which include songs with messages of hope in Christ. After laying down background tracks for one of my CDs, I found myself seated beside a beautiful woman who seemed a bit quiet and withdrawn. After the plane took off, she asked if I had family in Fort Wayne. "Thank you, Lord, for the open invitation for conversation." We talked briefly about my growing up in Fort Wayne and what I had been busy with in the studio on this trip. I asked if she was from Fort Wayne. She said, "No, I'm just passing through. I have had a very rough year and had to take care of some things." Then she put headphones on and proceeded to read a magazine, but that was all I needed to hear.

When the Holy Spirit prompts you to do something, say something, or share something, do it. When the plane landed, we stood up to get our onboard luggage. Quickly, I reached for a couple CDs and handed them to her. "May these provide comfort, peace, rest, and hope in Christ." She thanked me quickly and left. A few months later, I received a wonderful *heart-written* card thanking me for the CDs and sharing how much the messages in the songs meant to her. She also shared that she was a Christian and confided in me her testimony and the struggles she had been dealing with. I'm so thankful I listened and obeyed the prompt of God to encourage and comfort another.

Every time something like that happens, it's just me living out Rest In Him Ministry's theme verse: "Praise be to the God and Father of our Lord Jesus Christ, the Father of compassion and the God of all comfort, who comforts us in all our troubles, so that we can comfort those in any trouble with the comfort we ourselves have received from God" (2 Corinthians 1:3–4).

Paul and Barnabas
Encouraging others has a rich history in the life of the church.

When Paul was a new convert to Christianity (so new that he was still being called Saul), the disciples in Jerusalem didn't really trust him. After all, he had been persecuting Christians with all his energy. "When he came to Jerusalem, he tried to join the disciples, but they were all afraid of him, not believing that he really was a disciple. But Barnabas took him and brought him to the apostles. He told them how Saul on his journey had seen the Lord and that the Lord had spoken to him, and how in Damascus he had preached fearlessly in the name of Jesus" (Acts 9:26–27).

Imagine how Saul/Paul felt when Barnabas (whose name actually means "son of encouragement") risked his own reputation by standing up for Paul and confirming what the Lord had done and was doing through him.

Imagine how Barnabas, whose real name was Joseph, felt when he was given such a positive nickname (and how you will feel when you know you've been an encouragement to someone).

In the same way that God created more than one kind of tree and thousands of species of birds, he doesn't rely on just one way of encouraging his children.

Ways God Has Encouraged Me through His Word

"For everything that was written in the past was written to teach us, so that through the endurance taught in the Scriptures and the encouragement they provide we might have hope" (Romans 15:4).

The Psalms of David are an excellent example of how God encourages us through his word:

- When David rejoices in God's protection and peace, it encourages us to trust in God (Psalm 61).
- By crying out to God in his distress, David encourages us to praise God for helping him with his mighty power (Psalm 18).
- When David repents and asks God to be merciful, we are encouraged to also ask for forgiveness (Psalm 51).

- By asking God to give him direction, David encourages us to be patient (Psalm 25).
- When David grieves, it encourages us to cast all our cares on God (Psalm 31).

Ways God Has Encouraged Me through Others
- A loving husband who showed me who Jesus Christ is
- Children and grandchildren who both give and raise up within me unconditional love
- A Christian counselor who seems to speak more Scripture than words of his own
- Friends who pray and send cards of compassion and comfort
- The testimonies of others who have weathered storms
- Wise authors who have written books that are not only challenging but encouraging
- Songs of faith, ancient and modern

Why Do We Need to Encourage Others?
The simple answer to this question can be found in the children's chorus "Jesus Loves Me": "For the Bible tells me so."[33] For instance:
- "Strive for full restoration, encourage one another" (2 Corinthians 13:11).
- "Encourage one another and build each other up" (1 Thessalonians 5:11).

---

33. "Jesus Loves Me," Words and music by Anna Bartlett Warner and William Batchelder Bradbury, Public Domain.

- "And we urge you, brothers and sisters, warn those who are idle and disruptive, encourage the disheartened, help the weak, be patient with everyone" (1 Thessalonians 5:14).
- "Encourage one another daily" (Hebrews 3:13).

A less-simple answer is that we represent God's heart for people. God loves the world, and we must show the world the truth of that. "Jesus replied: '"Love the Lord your God with all your heart and with all your soul and with all your mind." This is the first and greatest commandment. And the second is like it: "Love your neighbor as yourself." All the Law and the Prophets hang on these two commandments'" (Matthew 22:37–40).

How Do We Encourage Others?

Here's where the Golden Rule really comes into play. As Stacy Wiebe wrote in "19 Ways to Encourage Others," "knowing what a big difference encouragement makes in your own life helps you know what you can do to encourage others."[34]

Pray

- With a quiet heart, pray for God's guidance.
- Pray for God to help you see the needs of people.
- Pray for God to help you listen to the needs of people.
- Pray for God to help you feel compassion for others.

---

34. Stacy Wiebe, "19 Ways to Encourage Others," https://thelife.com/19-ways-to-encourage-others.

- Pray for God to give you the ability to act, to *be* the encouragement.

Read

Read God's Word daily. You cannot share what you do not know, so prepare your heart with the knowledge of what Christ offers.

Listen and Watch

I find it helpful that the words *listen* and *silent* contain the same letters. That reminds me to listen and watch for clues about what the people I'm with need from God. I ask myself: Are their eyes downcast? Are there tears? What are they really saying, both with their words and their facial expressions?

Share

When they are ready and able to listen, concentrate on sharing compassion. I don't mean that you should deny or ignore their struggles, but your input should encourage them toward God's higher purposes. (And while it is always God's ultimate purpose that we will live in complete communion with him, there may be baby steps to take along the way, depending on what a person is dealing with.)

Are there songs, books, or specific Scriptures you could recommend?

Pray in the Moment

That's right, I'm saying it again. Pray for them right then, in the moment. Hearing someone say, "I'll be praying for you" is never as encouraging as hearing someone actually pray!

Later, follow up with a greeting card to let them know you still care.

Hospitality
Offer hospitality to one another without grumbling. Each of you should use whatever gift you have received to serve others, as faithful stewards of God's grace in its various forms. If anyone speaks, they should do so as one who speaks the very words of God. If anyone serves, they should do so with the strength God provides, so that in all things God may be praised through Jesus Christ. To him be the glory and the power for ever and ever. (1 Peter 4:9–11)

"Lord, as the storm subsides...
Help me to SEE Your sovereign, loving hand in it,
and let my song of PRAISE to You echo throughout the ages,
from generation to generation. TELLING of
Your faithful love, Your awesome deeds . . . that I might
have the privilege and joy of sharing the hope I found
in You with others in needs."[35]

Ripples
How have others encouraged you?

Rewrite the psalms cited in this chapter in your own words and for your own circumstances (Psalms 18, 25, 31, 51, and 61).

---

35. Sandi Banks, *Anchors of Hope* (Nashville: Broadman & Holman Publishers, 2002), 118.

Perhaps this piece I wrote for a presentation (also titled "Sweet Encouragement") will ring true for you:

God shows me strength when I am weak.
God shows me compassion while I suffer.
God reassures me with hope and I survive.
God loves me even through my sin.
God provides peace as I experience loss.
God wraps me in arms of rest in the midst of sorrow.
God comforts me during troubles.
Therefore,
I will share His
strength and compassion,
hope, love, peace,
rest and comfort.

When thinking about sharing our own stories along with God's story, my producer had the wisdom to combine two classic hymns.

Amazing Grace/I Love to Tell the Story

Amazing grace, how sweet the sound
That saved a wretch like me
I once was lost but now am found
Was blind, but now I see

I love to tell the story
'Twill be my theme in glory
To tell the old, old story
Of Jesus and His love

I love to tell the story of unseen things above
Of Jesus and His glory, of Jesus and His love
I love to tell the story, because I know 'tis true
It satisfied my longings as nothing else would do

I love to tell the story for those who know it best
Seem hungering and thirsting to hear it like the rest
And when in scenes of glory I sing the new, new song
'Twill be the old, old story that I have loved so long

I love to tell the story
'Twill be my theme in glory
To tell the old, old story
Of Jesus and His love

When we've been there ten thousand years
Bright shining as the sun
We've no less days to sing God's praise
Than when we'd first begun[36]

---

36. "Amazing Grace/I Love to Tell the Story," Public Domain. Arrangement © 2011 Chet A. Chambers. Used by permission. Words and Music John Newton/A. Katherine Hankey, performed by Debbie Roth on *living letters of HOPE.*

1 | 2

Sharing God's Love: Living Letters of Hope

A sunbeam, a sunbeam,
Jesus wants me for a sunbeam.
A sunbeam, a sunbeam,
I'll be a sunbeam for Him.

—Nellie Talbot

Once upon a time, a little girl attended a big church in the city. She would go downstairs, attend a class with friends, and always sing a song about sunbeams. When class ended, everyone would go up the stairs into a large room that had long wooden benches. There were books in holders on the back of the next bench, and she enjoyed picking at the foam at the bottom of the holders, which was meant to keep the books from being too loud when they were put back after the singing was over. When everyone stopped talking at the front of the big room, she knew it was time to go home and have fried chicken for lunch.

Those are my memories from attending church as a child—that's about it! However, I never forgot that song about sunbeams. Little did I know that at age nineteen I would make a decision to follow Jesus Christ and make him my Lord and Savior. It was a while before I learned what being a sunbeam for Jesus was all about, but God gently took me by the hand and heart and showed me.

Do his rays of "love, joy, peace, patience, kindness, goodness, faithfulness, gentleness, and self-control" shine through you (Galatians 5:22–23 NLT)?

We can think about our public influence as sunbeams or like ripples in the water. We are moving from being drenched in the storms and struggles to drenched in hope. Beauty from the inside will shine on the outside. A reflection of all God is doing *in* you will emanate *from* you and affect those *around* you. "Those who look to [God] are radiant; their faces are never covered with shame" (Psalm 34:5).

We are the carriers of the good news. If my life is a "sunbeam for Jesus," then I need to tell my story. But how? Let's use the apostle Paul's example as an outline to help us organize our own stories.

Paul's Testimony

I am a Jew, born in Tarsus of Cilicia, but brought up in this city. I studied under Gamaliel and was thoroughly trained in the law of our ancestors. I was just as zealous for God as any of you are today. I persecuted the followers of this Way to their death, arresting both men and women and throwing them into prison, as the high priest and all the Council can themselves testify. I even obtained letters from them to their associates in Damascus, and went there to bring these people as prisoners to Jerusalem to be punished.

About noon as I came near Damascus, suddenly a bright light from heaven flashed around me. I fell to the ground and heard a voice say to me, "Saul! Saul! Why do you persecute me?"

"Who are you, Lord?" I asked.

"I am Jesus of Nazareth, whom you are persecuting," he replied. My companions saw the light, but they did not understand the voice of him who was speaking to me.

"What shall I do, Lord?" I asked.

"Get up," the Lord said, "and go into Damascus. There you will be told all that you have been assigned to do." My companions led me by the hand into Damascus, because the brilliance of the light had blinded me.

A man named Ananias came to see me. He was a devout observer of the law and highly respected by all the Jews living there. He stood beside me and said, "Brother Saul, receive your sight!" And at that very moment I was able to see him.

Then he said: "The God of our ancestors has chosen you to know his will and to see the Righteous One and to hear words from his mouth. You will be his witness to all people of what you have seen and heard. And now what are you waiting for? Get up, be baptized and wash your sins away, calling on his name."

When I returned to Jerusalem and was praying at the temple, I fell into a trance and saw the Lord speaking to me. "Quick!" he said. "Leave Jerusalem immediately, because the people here will not accept your testimony about me."

"Lord," I replied, "these people know that I went from one synagogue to another to imprison and beat those who believe in you. And when the blood of your martyr Stephen was shed, I stood there giving my approval and guarding the clothes of those who were killing him."

Then the Lord said to me, "Go; I will send you far away to the Gentiles." (Acts 22:3–21)

An Outline for Our Stories

Paul's testimony follows a simple outline that countless people have used to tell their stories concisely and understandably.

Who I Was before Meeting Jesus

Paul talked about his upbringing and how he persecuted Christians. For me, this part is a tale of abuse, promiscuity, and self-hatred.

What about you? There's no need to glorify the sins of the past, but an acknowledgement of your wrong actions and attitudes is appropriate.

How I Met Jesus

Not everyone's story will be as dramatic as Paul's or involve musical theater and a future husband like mine, but there most certainly will be details of people, places, and events God used to draw you to himself.

Who I Am Now That I've Met Jesus

Accepting Jesus must involve some kind of change to our lives. Jesus didn't only die so that our sins could be forgiven. He also rose from the dead so we could have brand-new lives. "I have come that they may have life, and have it to the full" (John 10:10). We are not just saved *from* something; we are also saved *for* something.

What difference has Jesus made in your life?

And don't misunderstand. This isn't a "Jesus said we were to be his witnesses" kind of strict obedience thing. We need to tell our stories because *people need to hear them.* It is truly encouraging to know that someone else has made it through a storm that's similar to the one you're getting drenched by, isn't it? Well then, shouldn't we pass on that encouragement to others?

Of course we should.

Ripples

Sincerely pray the "Prayer of Saint Francis" and write out your own story. Then get ready for God to give you opportunities to be a living letter of hope to those around you!

Prayer of Saint Francis

Lord, make me an instrument of your peace;
where there is hatred, let me sow love;
where there is injury, pardon;
where there is doubt, faith;
where there is despair, hope;
where there is darkness, light;
and where there is sadness, joy.

O Divine Master,
grant that I may not so much seek to be consoled as
to console;
to be understood, as to understand;
to be loved, as to love;
for it is in giving that we receive,

it is in pardoning that we are pardoned,
and it is in dying that we are born to Eternal Life.
Amen.[37]

What a privilege to be able to sing this song with confidence and peace.

My Hope

I know God is good
I know I can trust Him every day
He provides for me in every way
He is faithful and He's true
Each morning His mercies are brand-new
How deep, how high, how wide is the love of God

Jesus is my Hope, my Salvation, my Redeemer
My Savior, and my King, my faithful Friend
He'll keep me from falling
Through His word and the Spirit's calling

When I put my trust in Him
Jesus is my Hope[38]

---

37. While these words are attributed to Saint Francis of Assissi, no one really knows their authorship. One of the places they can be found online is https://www.stfrancis.edu/prayer-of-st-francis.
38. "My Hope," © 2011 Chet A. Chambers, Nathan Heironimus. Used by permission. Words and Music Chet Chambers and Nathan Heironimus, performed by Debbie Roth on *living letters of HOPE*.

Afterword

Praise be to the God and Father of our Lord Jesus Christ! In his great mercy he has given us new birth into a living hope through the resurrection of Jesus Christ from the dead, and into an inheritance that can never perish, spoil or fade. This inheritance is kept in heaven for you, who through faith are shielded by God's power until the coming of the salvation that is ready to be revealed in the last time. In all this you greatly rejoice, though now for a little while you may have had to suffer grief in all kinds of trials. These have come so that the proven genuineness of your faith—of greater worth than gold, which perishes even though refined by fire—may result in praise, glory and honor when Jesus Christ is revealed. Though you have not seen him, you love him; and even though you do not see him now, you believe in him and are filled with an inexpressible and glorious joy, for you are receiving the end result of your faith, the salvation of your souls. (1 Peter 1:3–9)

Jesus answered, "Everyone who drinks this water will be thirsty again, but whoever drinks the water I give them will never thirst. Indeed, the water I give them will become in them a spring of water welling up to eternal life" (John 4:13–14).

Drenched – *adj.* containing, covered with, or thoroughly penetrated by water. *Synonyms*: awash, bedraggled, doused, dripping, saturated, soaked, soggy, sopping, waterlogged.[39]

Being drenched in those ways certainly isn't a pleasant experience. Being drenched in struggles and pain isn't either, of course. But I hope the word *drenched* now has a positive bent to it for you. Troubles are bound to come, but if you can hang on to hope when they do, you will find that being drenched in the love of our Lord is our only hope in the storm.

Therefore, the next time you are caught in a storm and drenched in struggles, sing in the rain and become drenched in survival. When the rain subsides, consider yourself drenched in hope and splash in the puddles. And when the rainbow comes out, share with others how you became drenched in the *Son*shine.

---

39. https://www.merriam-webster.com/thesaurus/drenched.

Recommended Reading

For a deeper knowledge about some of the topics I've touched on in *Drenched*, I recommend the following books:

Banks, Sandi. *Anchors of Hope.* Nashville, TN: Broadman & Holman Publishers, 2002.

Boom, Corrie ten. *The Hiding Place.* New York: Inspirational Press, 1971.

Gerber, Charles R. *Christ-Centered Self-Esteem.* Joplin, MO: College Press Publishing Company, 1996.

———. *Healing for a Bitter Heart.* Joplin, MO: College Press Publishing Company, 1996.

Higgs, Liz Curtis. *Embrace Grace.* Colorado Springs, CO: WaterBrook Press, 2006.

Kent, Carol. *When I Lay My Isaac Down.* Colorado Springs, CO: NavPress, 2004.

Lloyd, Natalie. *Paperdoll.* Ventura, CA: Regal, 2009.

Lotz, Anne Graham. *Why?* Nashville, TN: W Publishing Group, 2004.

Lucado, Max. *God's Inspirational Promise Book.* Nashville, TN: J. Countryman, 1996.

———. *Come Thirsty.* Nashville, TN: W Publishing Group, 2004.

———. *God's Story Your Story.* Grand Rapids, MI: Zondervan, 2011.

———. *Grace.* Nashville, TN: Thomas Nelson, 2012.

———. *It's Not About Me.* Brentwood, TN: Integrity Publishers, 2004.

Nicodem, James L. *Prayer Coach.* Wheaton, IL: Crossway Books, 2008.

Walsh, Sheila. *In the Middle of the Mess.* Nashville, TN: Thomas Nelson, 2017.

Whiting, Karen. *365 Devotions for Hope.* Grand Rapids, MI: Zondervan, 2015.

Wood, Christine, *Character Witness.* Madison, WI: InterVarsity Press, 2003.

GIVING THANKS:

Drenched in Gratitude

Writing and publishing a book is never an individual effort, and I'm overflowing with gratitude for the following:

God the Father, his Son Jesus Christ, and the perfect Counselor, the Holy Spirit: Thank you for your comfort, peace, love, and eternal hope. Without you, I wouldn't be alive.

Dewey: Thank you for your compassionate eyes, arms of love, introducing Jesus to a messed up nineteen-year-old, and staying beside me no matter what.

Angel, Shonda, Curtis, and Kelly Jo: Thank you for loving your mommy.

Charley Gerber: Thank you for your faithful encouragement and biblical wisdom over the years when I was feeling like a broken ragdoll.

Chet Chambers: Thank you for your beautiful lyrics and music, which captured what my heart felt. May your words that appear in this book be continued comfort for the readers.

Redemption Press—Thank you, Athena, for obeying God and sending the message of encouragement to write this book. Thanks also to your team for nurturing me through the process of writing for the first time.

Thanks also to the following friends who generously gave toward the financial needs of this project:

Kari Altema

Gwen Arbuckle

Les & Daralee Baker

Scott & Cheri Besser

Bob & Tara Bower

Teri Boyden

Marcelle Bright

Bob & Connie Brown

Jodi Byland

Roland & Mary Alice
  Denney

Kirk & Teresa Douglas

Larry Fortier

Steve & Julie Ginader

Steve & Claudia Glinski

Kevin & Denise Hall

John & Shannon
  Hammar

Dick Hanson

Roger & Claryce Haug

John & Christina Jaeger

Sue Kretchmer

Larry McCaghy

Andy & Ami McClure

Jennifer Merhar

Roger & Barb Miller

Don & Luann Moe

Terry & Diane
  Munsinger

Betty Ormsby

Eric Peltoniemi

Thelma Peters

Jan Rokosz

Phil Shafer

Todd & Jeanne Sjoquist

Phillip & Angel Stanley

Ted & Kathren Tellman

Chuck & Jody Thiesfeld

Steve & Cheri Twiss

Ginger Venugopal

Derrel & Sharon Warner

Becky Watczak

Kathryn Williamson

Mark Wilson

Kim Wittek

How to Hear the Songs

If you would like to have any or all of the four CDs mentioned in *Drenched*, they are available on a "whatever you can afford" basis. I have never charged a set fee for my speaking engagements or my music, and God has always provided for my needs. Please contact me by email: debbie@RestIn-HimMinistry.com. (Donations can be made online by sending money to debbie@RestInHimMinistry.com through PayPal, or you can write a check to "Rest In Him Ministry" and mail it to Debbie Roth, 16715 Gannon Ave W, Rosemount, MN 55068.)

To hear the specific songs quoted in this book, go to soundcloud.com/debbieroth.

About the Author

Debbie Roth is the founder of Rest in Him Ministry as well as a paraprofessional who works in a transitional school for young adults with special needs. A vocal coach, singer, speaker, author, wife, mother, and grandmother, Debbie lives in Rosemount, Minnesota, with her husband and two dogs.

Debbie began Rest In Him Ministry as a way to turn the miseries she has experienced in her life into a ministry of hope and restoration. She has been comforting others with the comfort she has received from God (2 Corinthians 1:3–4) at retreats, banquets, and worship services since 2005.

To learn more, please visit
www.RestInHimMinistry.com.
To contact Debbie, please email
Debbie@RestInHimMinistry.com.

Order Information

REDEMPTION PRESS

To order additional copies of this book, please visit
www.redemption-press.com.
Also available on Amazon.com and BarnesandNoble.com
Or by calling toll free 1-844-2REDEEM.

Drenched

ONLY
HOPE
IN THE
Storm

Drenched

ONLY
HOPE
IN THE
Storm

II Cor 1:3,4

Debbie Roth

DEBBIE ROTH

REDEMPTION
PRESS